Playing in the Dust

Playing in the Dust

A Pilgrimage with the Creation Stories

David Runcorn

CANTERBURY
PRESS
Norwich

© David Runcorn 2024

Published in 2024 by Canterbury Press
Editorial office
3rd Floor, Invicta House,
110 Golden Lane,
London EC1Y 0TG, UK

www.canterburypress.co.uk

Canterbury Press is an imprint of Hymns Ancient & Modern Ltd
(a registered charity)

HYMNS Ancient
&Modern

Hymns Ancient & Modern® is a registered trademark of
Hymns Ancient & Modern Ltd
13A Hellesdon Park Road, Norwich,
Norfolk NR6 5DR, UK

Unless otherwise stated in the text, scripture quotations are from the New
Revised Standard Version Bible: Anglicized Edition, copyright © 1989, 1995
National Council of the Churches of Christ in the United States of America.
Used by permission. All rights reserved worldwide.
Scripture quotations marked 'NIV' are taken from the Holy Bible, New
International Version®, NIV®. Copyright © 1973, 1978, 1984, 2011
by Biblica, Inc.™ Used by permission of Zondervan. All rights reserved
worldwide. www.zondervan.com The 'NIV' and 'New International
Version' are trademarks registered in the United States Patent and
Trademark Office by Biblica, Inc.™
Scripture quotations marked 'The Message' are taken from The Message.
Copyright 1993, 1994, 1995, 1996, 2000, 2001, 2002.
Used by permission of NavPress Publishing Group.
Scripture quotations marked 'KJV' are from the Authorized Version
of the Bible (The King James Bible), the rights in which are vested in
the Crown, are reproduced by permission of the Crown's Patentee,
Cambridge University Press.

British Library Cataloguing in Publication data

A catalogue record for this book is available
from the British Library

ISBN: 978-1-78622-629-7

Typeset by Regent Typesetting

'In the Scriptures we are in our Father's house
where the children are permitted to play.'
Raymond Brown

'Yahweh created me at the beginning of his work
... when he laid the foundations of the Earth.
Then I was with him as the apple of his eye
and I was daily his joy;
constantly playing before his face,
playing in his inhabited world,
and rejoicing in humankind.'
From Proverbs 8.22–31

'In the beginning was the conversation.'
John 1.1 Erasmus

to Jackie
for all beginning now

Contents

About the book cover

In religious art it is rare to find depictions of Adam and Eve that are not preoccupied with temptation, sin or their anguished eviction from the garden of Eden. The cover chosen for this book is one exception. It is a painting by the Finnish artist Hugo Simberg (d. 1917). He called it *Paratiisi*, – Paradise.

Some artists, like some storytellers, make their meaning clear. Others let the picture speak and so leave spaces for personal interpretation. *Paratiisi* is more of the latter as, I think, are the creation stories.

The scene Simberg has painted has both simplicity and depth, like the story it is exploring. Creation has a new and unfinished feel. In the background, the trees are in harvest mode, but the foreground is bare and unadorned.

In the centre of the picture is a companionable triangulation of God, Eve and Adam. On the ground before them, a bead game is laid out, ready to play. Eve is leaning forward. Her right hand is reaching into the dust. She is looking at Adam with eager intent. In another Bible context this might be the lively presence of divine wisdom, personified through the wholly positive image of a woman. Meanwhile, God is also gazing upon Adam, with steady, non-anxious curiosity.

The moment is poised.

We are waiting for something to happen.

Where is Adam in all this? His eyes are shut, his head lifted. Is he concentrating or just unconscious? Here is humanity, yet to awaken – to itself, to life, to companionship, and to God.

We are surely at that moment in the picture.

All is ready.

My hope is that the reflections that follow capture the same spirit of beginning, of play, awakening, and of endless possibility.

Let Me Tell You a Story

Some introductions

Sitting opposite me on the train, a young boy was curled up in his seat, almost hidden behind the large book he was gripping hard with his small hands. It was called *Megamonster*. He was oblivious to all around him and so captivated by what he was reading that he was physically leaning into the book as if to get nearer the action.

Our lives begin with stories. We are born into them. From our earliest moments we are surrounded by them. Bedtime stories are one of my earliest memories as a child. Bathed, cuddled up, warm and content at the end of the day, they were part of love, life and home and a doorway into worlds I had yet to discover. The invitation to make believe, to playfully explore with unbounded imagination is what gives us the framework for our journeys into life and for acquiring the essential life skills for managing monsters. The Bible calls this wisdom. Repetition was part of the fun. 'Read it again!' But I was often asleep before the end. Years later, I watched those stories weave their magic on my children too.

That the beginning of the Bible finds God telling us stories is significant. In biblical and theological studies there has been a rediscovery of story and a renewed focus on the Bible as literature. Close textual analysis is still important. But the realization has slowly dawned that if the ancient scribes have gone to the trouble of carefully crafting those texts and words into stories it is not really our task to take them apart and 'explain' them.

I was not expecting to write this book. It emerged out of a period of my life when I was struggling with exhaustion. Not surprisingly, faith too had become a wilderness. The familiar texts, prayers and disciplines of a lifetime now felt empty of meaning. You may have known such times? I continued to practise and explore faith as best I knew how – particularly through the preaching, writing, talks, Bible studies and retreat reflections that have always been my ministry. On the occasions when the subject was mine to choose, I invariably turned to the creation stories. Something always seemed to be going on there, stirring in the dark. So, when I was invited to speak at a holiday week at Scargill House[1] I opted again for the opening chapters of the Bible. As I spoke, I found myself energized in new ways by those familiar words and images. It felt as if faith was being recreated. The experience seemed to be mutual. Each morning, after offering a Bible reflection, I invited any who wished to talk further to return after the coffee break. I expected a few to come, for half an hour or so. *Everyone* came. Every day. They became exhilarating times of communal Bible reading, theological exploration, honest questioning, and personal storytelling that only stopped when it was time for lunch. This book is my continued conversation out of that journey shared and the themes that surfaced over those days. So wherever life and faith finds you as you read this, please hear the invitation to join in.

This book takes the form of short reflections that travel alongside, and circle around, the Bible stories, pausing occasionally to take time with particular themes or insights. I have tried to sit close to the storyteller. I am hearing-impaired so I am used to having to listen carefully and to keep checking. The stories had a way of continually surprising me. I thought I knew them so well. Someone wisely observed that you can never read them too *slowly*. I have imagined being in conversation with the storyteller. 'What do you mean?' ... 'I don't understand' ... 'How does that make sense?' All the time I have tried to trust where those stories might lead and what it might mean to be building faith upon them. We do not listen well when we are fearful or anxious, and in the many challenges the church is presently facing there is a great deal of both.

---

1 https://scargillmovement.org, accessed 25.07.2024

Each chapter is therefore incomplete in a sense. Perhaps we are always closer to the beginning of the conversation than the end. Short as they are, these stories of our creation prove to be inexhaustible and the discussion can, and does, continue in a variety of directions.

We never read the Bible in a vacuum. We come to it laden with our own questions, experiences, concerns and needs. We also come with blind spots and assumptions that have been shaping our understanding without being aware of it. The creation stories in the Bible are burdened more than most with all these. The first task is to try to be as aware as we can of what we bring, and then to lay them down. Not because they do not matter, or are unwelcome but because, if the text is to guide us, we must first let it speak on its own terms, in its own way, with its own twists and turns and quirky strangeness. That is the way stories work, especially when God is telling them.

Just a word about my writing style. There are no non-gendered personal pronouns in English. For reasons that I hope will be clear as we go along, I have tried to reduce the number of references to God and the first human as 'he', except where it is appropriate, and without sounding as if I am trying to make a point.

The Bible text of the two stories are printed at the end of the book. I encourage you to read them through as a whole, perhaps more than once, as you journey with this book.

So if you are ready, let's begin ...

I

Beginning Now

Creating then and now

In the beginning God created the heavens and the earth ...
(Gen. 1.1)

All stories start somewhere.

In the Bible it is 'In the beginning'. Those iconic opening words have the capacity to tip us back, in imagination, wonder and faith, into the mystery of our absolute origins. Two things are clear at the outset.

This world is the creation of God.

We are, therefore, creatures. 'To be a creature is to know that you are not the source of your own life but must constantly receive it from the varying forms of births, nurture, healing, inspiration, and kinship' (Wirzba, 2021, p. xviii). Our primary source is God. And that is where the Bible starts.

That opening declaration is in the past tense in our Bibles. God created. So we tend to read it as describing a completed action, back in the past. Job done. If you look in the footnotes at the bottom of that first page of your Bible, though, you will likely find an alternative reading suggested there. 'In the beginning when God *began creating* ...' Bible footnotes are always in very small print. They are easily missed, and the impression is given that they offer a less important or reliable option. This means that the alternative reading of the first verse of the Bible is rarely read aloud.

How might our understanding have changed if that footnoted translation had been the default version in the text? Try reading it aloud.

In the beginning when God *began creating* the heavens and the earth ...

There is now an energy and movement in the text, don't you think? It is now a creating that continues into the *present*. Something that began back then is still at work. Everything that was in the beginning is still beginning *now*. Even the light of the stars in the night sky is continually arriving from the beginning.

We might wonder who chose the default version? Why was a stress on a past action felt to be more theologically important? It tends to leave the focus on a finished product rather than on a continuing process. But creation is a process. In fact, the default version is found in the earliest complete English Bible translations of John Wycliffe, Myles Coverdale and William Tyndale. The ancient storyteller was not making that choice at all, however. Both alternatives are needed to capture the fullest sense of what the story is declaring. Every work of translation is an attempt at faithful interpretation. We always need to keep in mind that the most literal reading will not always be the most accurate one. It may even be completely misleading.

It is therefore a misunderstanding to ask which version is 'true'. They both are. God is the original source of this world. But this universe is not something completed and signed off. Life is continually evolving and emerging. We are unfinished, and perhaps better described as human becomers than human beings. God is still at work. As Psalm 104 puts it, 'You send forth your spirit and life begins. You renew the face of the earth' (v. 30). There is no end to the creating life of an eternal God.

It has been said that life revolves around variations on three questions:

Where are you?
Who are you?
How should you live? (Wirzba, 2021, p. x)

The answers to those questions will always, at some point, require us to go searching through our beginnings – the story into which we were born and why. We return to our beginnings because we need them, and for reasons far more important than curiosity or scientific theories about our origins. That is exactly what the Bible is guiding us to in its opening pages. Knowing our beginnings gives us a sense of what our lives are based on. It gives our life a foundation of meaning, of purpose – and therefore direction.

Though the Bible has little interest in the abstract theories of our beginnings, it does insist on the need to remember. This is never more needed, and therefore urged, than in times of uncertainty, pain and loss. 'Remember me,' says God, 'Remember Torah,' 'Remember your story,' 'Teach your children to remember' (for example: Isa. 46.9; Deut. 24.9; Ps. 42.4, 6). This remembering is not about having a good memory for dates and names. Nor is it looking back over our shoulder to some imagined or longed-for past. We can and do get hopelessly stuck doing that. Remembering is about living deeply with what makes us who we are now.

Through the repetition of that remembering we never leave the past behind. It is present to us.

The timeline of our personal story is, for the greater part, unknowable to us of course. But an informed awareness of where we have come from and the stories we have been part of, for good or ill, are a basic human need. It is not surprising, particularly in uncertain times, that resources for tracing ancestry and family trees are in such demand. *Long Lost Families* is a perennially popular television programme that assists people in their search for unknown forebears. It is abundantly clear how deeply this matters to people. Their very selves are tied up in this search. Without it, people simply feel lost. When relatives are traced and stories revealed, people speak of a sense of completion and belonging.

A story of our beginnings is as much about who we are now and where we are going. In its very first words the Bible reveals how well it understands our need. Meg Warner has memorably called the book of Genesis 'a past for a people in need of a future' (2024).

2

God

The God who makes things

In the beginning, God ... (Gen. 1.1)

What kind of God makes things?

The answer is not immediately obvious. God is fullness itself, the All in All, and so has no need of anything or anyone else. God lacks nothing. There is no job to be done or project that needs a workforce. God is not motivated out of want or seeks anything out of jealousy or possessiveness. That would not even occur to him. In any case there isn't anything that is other than God to desire. Nor did God create Adam and Eve out of loneliness (as more than one children's Bible book has claimed).

All of which means that creation is, by any familiar measure of things, completely pointless.

Here in the beginning, the God who makes things is revealed by what he creates and is made known by the way he does so. Three things are immediately clear as this creation story unfolds.

First, the world that is coming into being is the sovereign work and will of God. It would not exist otherwise. This revelation is the bedrock of all life and attempts to live apart from this truth are invariably disastrous.

Second, creation is not a remote, impersonal action. A God who speaks and personally crafts a world into existence is a God who communicates and seeks relationship with it. To whom is he speaking in this story? In parts of the Bible, such as the beginning of Job, God is surrounded by a heavenly council. Perhaps he is speaking to them? Or does his speaking at the beginning of creation, as yet without anyone to hear or respond, declare his intention for creation to find voice to reply with?

Third, creation is being allowed to come into being and have its own life. We are being given to ourselves, to be ourselves. God leaves us free. It is all gift.

The Hebrew word used for 'create' is only found here in the Bible (vv. 1, 21 and 27) and only with reference to God's creating. It means 'to create without effort'. In the myths of surrounding nations creation was a battlefield in a continual power struggle between the gods. The God of the Hebrews is outside all that. The focus here is not on divine power, however. That is without question. The story is telling us *how* that power is expressed and what kind of world emerges when such power is life-giving.

But how does an eternal God, who is the fullness of all things everywhere, find a space anywhere for anything else to freely exist at all? The medieval rabbis pondered long over this and decided God did the equivalent of sucking in his stomach. For creation to be possible at all requires God to withdraw in some way. Creation involves a divine self-limiting, a holding-back – without which nothing could exist that is other than God. In this sense, creation is not a work of supreme power so much as a movement of divine self-emptying. In that spaciousness, all this comes into being – life, that by divine permission, is *not* God. God not only creates this world, he gives it substantial space and freedom to make itself.

Had women been included in the rabbis' debates (and generally they were not), the discussion might naturally have found an illustration in the way space for human life to grow is made, with infinite, tender vulnerability, in the womb of a mother. Does this image helpfully represent our creation in God? The theologian Jürgen Moltmann seems to affirm this when he writes that God has 'created a world "in himself", giving it time *in* his eternity, finitude *in* his infinity, space *in* his omnipresence, and freedom *in* his selfless love' (Moltmann, 1981, p. 109).

If God has no particular reason or need to create, then this must all be a gift of love. Creation comes into being through a gratuitous outpouring of divine love, out of the desire of God to be giving. For that is what God is like. 'God had to create a universe', writes J. V. Taylor. 'It was in the nature of things that

8

God should do so, not because God needed anything beyond God, but because love is more than satisfying need, more than necessity' (1992, p. 195).

St Paul directs the faithful to use the example of Christ's humility as their role model. 'Let the same mind be in you that was in Christ Jesus,' he urged. What was he particularly emphasizing? It was the way that Christ, 'Though he was in the form of God, did not regard equality with God as something to be exploited but emptied himself' (Phil. 2.5–6). But why would he exploit this at all? It would not even occur to him to behave like that. A clearer sense of that verse would be to say, '*Precisely because* he was in the form of God he did not exploit.' God does not exploit. This world is the gift of a self-emptying, non-possessive God. This world comes into being not because of God's overwhelming power or will. Creation is not a work of self-interest at all. We are here because God is humble.

The fourth-century saint Isaac the Syrian called humility 'the garment of divinity'. There is no contradiction between the idea of a God who is all-powerful and one who is humble. Humility is about not exploiting power to one's own advantage. Humility is not the surrender of power so much as the way that power is offered and expressed. We easily misunderstand this and think humility means self-negation before God, required because God is Almighty, holy and all powerful. Following St Paul, Isaac is saying we are to be clothed in humility *precisely because* we are made in the image of a humble God.

Karen Keen has written a very helpful book on the origins, inspiration and interpretation of the Bible. She calls it *The Word of a Humble God* (2022). The title reminds us that the scriptures themselves are the revelation of the same serving, self-surrendering love through which this world comes to birth. The scriptures too make space for us. They are to be opened and read in humility and joy together, as they reveal God the creator and his life and ways in the world.

3

Tohu wa Bohu

Out of the void

The earth was a formless void and darkness covered the face of the deep, while a wind from God swept over the face of the waters. (Gen. 1.2)

The world does not appear out of nothing in Genesis. Something is present but what exactly this may be is unclear. The Hebrew words are actually untranslatable – *'tohu wa bohu'*. Various translators' versions are on offer. 'Empty non-being'. 'Shapeless flux'. 'Welter and waste'. My favourite is 'a soup of nothingness', which resonates well with cosmologists who speak of soups of gases and particles when describing the origins of stars and planets. Perhaps the phrase is meant to be as meaningless as it sounds, because what is going on is chaotically inexpressible.

Although this ancient story is placed first in the Bible it is thought to have emerged in its final form at the far end of Israel's history. In 597 BC Israel was conquered by the armies of Babylon, and a large part of the population taken into exile. This was far more than just a military disaster. It was a spiritual and theological catastrophe. Even their God had apparently been defeated by foreign gods. Their land, Holy City and Temple had been laid waste, and every validating symbol and sign of their faith had been reduced to *'tohu wa bohu'*. As the prophet Jeremiah anguished over that scene at the time, he used the same words and images as this passage in Genesis. 'I looked on the earth, and lo, it was formless and void (*tohu wa bohu*) and to the heavens, and they had no light' (Gen. 4.23). His world has tipped back into non-creation. We are at the beginning again.

So this is where it all starts. The storyteller is already at the limits of his vocabulary. His imagination is at full stretch and beyond. Nothing is actually explained, for the simple reason that it cannot be. The void is shrouded in deep and total darkness. Alongside this are 'the waters'. In this detail ancient wisdom aligns with contemporary scientific knowledge. Life first emerged from water.

Over the waters something seems to be stirring.

Translating continues to be an uncertain task. What was stirring exactly? 'God's Spirit brooded like a bird above the watery abyss' expresses the most familiar attempts at translation (1.2, The Message). That image offers a reassuring sense of maternal care and nurturing. It is not at all clear that the reference to God's Spirit here is to be understood as the Holy Spirit of later revelation, however. Not least because it seems to play no further part in the creation account. Other translators hear a very different mood. One reads this as 'a wind from God swept over the face of the waters' (NRSVA). The theologian Gerhard von Rad insists the word 'brood' should not be the translation at all. The word 'brood' actually means vibrate, tremble or stir. It is also more than just a wind too, he says. This is a *storm* from God (von Rad, 1972, p. 49)! He has a point because the same word is used to describe Jeremiah in his extreme mental distress. 'My heart is crushed within me; all my bones *shake*' (Jer. 23.9, my italic).

The whole scene is altogether wilder and more turbulent than commonly read. Modern science would agree. When quantum physics tries to describe the state of matter it uses words like shaking, pulsing, twisting, curling waves and jittering. The whole thing is vibrating – vulnerably and explosively alive.

How are we to read that movement over the waters then? Is this a maternal image of bringing to birth, or of wild storms? In fact, both senses of the word are found in a passage in Deuteronomy, where it is used to describe God's care of his people in their wilderness wanderings. In this passage Jacob is the collective ancestral name for God's people.

God 'sustained him [Jacob] in a desert land,
    in a howling wilderness waste;
he shielded him, cared for him,
    guarded him as the apple of his eye.
As an eagle stirs up its nest,
    and *hovers* over its young;
as it spreads its wings, takes them up,
    and bears them aloft on its pinions,
the Lord alone guided him.' (Deut. 32.10–12, my italic)

The passage is full of the language of guarding and protection in hazardous terrain. God cares for his people like the parent eagle, which hovers above and beneath its young as they learn to fly. But it is a firm and vigorous love. Why does the eagle stir up its eyrie? To tip its young out into those howling winds. It is to provoke them into entering the life that is theirs. Maternal brooding is not tame!

Back in the Genesis story, something is on the move. Out of that turbulent, jittering nothingness a unique work of creation is about to begin. As we have already seen, for the ancient Hebrew people telling stories of their beginnings is not simply to remember their past. It is to understand the present. For what was true then is still true now. To God's exiles, sifting over the rubble and *tohu wa bohu* of their lost life and faith, this is so improbably hopeful.

The message is this. God does his creating working with what is *tohu wah bohu*.

He still does.

As this story of creation unfolds,

chaos takes order and form,
emptiness finds substance,
'nothing' finds meaning,
what is untranslatable finds halting words and expression.

A new world is coming into being.
God needs no other material to do the work he loves most.
Chaos will do fine.
This is such good news!

4

'Let There Be'

The sound of God's voice

And God said, 'Let there be ...' And it was so. (Gen. 1.6, 7)

My father was a parish priest and whenever Genesis chapter 1 came around in the cycle of readings for public worship, he always assigned a particular man in the congregation to read it. This man was of very great age and had a powerful, authoritative bearing. But it was the voice I remember. When he read Genesis the sound seemed to come out of some deep, primordial depths. 'In the beginning ...' There in the choir stalls the hairs on the back of my neck stood up, and the ground beneath my feet almost trembled. I could believe he had watched it happen. For years afterwards I could only hear Genesis 1 through a voice that spoke of awesome power, effortless will and absolute, majestic authority.

Creation is the work of the One God. There were no competing gods or powers to fight off, or awkward neighbours to placate. No planning permission was needed. Creation emerges out of God's sovereign desire, free choice, gift and delight – and God's alone.

That this world comes into being through an exercise of supreme will, power and authority is not in itself good news, however. In today's world all too many live under oppressive powers and authoritarian regimes, just as nations did in times past. In the creation myths of the nations that surrounded Israel, humans lived in this world under divine tyranny and abject servitude. They were created to serve the insatiable needs and competing ambitions of the gods. Israel's story stands in utter contrast to all that. A quite different way of expressing will, power and authority is being revealed through this creating act. Rather than being an impressive demonstration of dominant, overwhelming, despotic power, creation is coming into being through a generous act of divine self-surrender, as we saw in Chapter 2. Power, reputation and status are of no interest to a God who is humble.

Scripture is never univocal. The task of interpreting it also requires listening to a variety of voices. The wisdom we seek will be found in a mixture of all of them. That means it is always a bit of an experiment.

Good storytellers leave hints and clues along the way for their hearers to pick up and ponder over as the plot reveals and conceals by turns. In the Bible one of these hints is found in the way that the first words spoken by a lead character reveal something significant at the heart of their character or destiny. This can be a quality, a flaw, or potentially either. For example, Saul's first words were 'Let us turn back' (1 Sam. 9.5). And so it proved. His inability to see things through faithfully was his fatal flaw as a man and a king. By contrast Samuel's first words were, 'Here I am' (1 Sam 3.4ff). And so he was. He is revered today in the three historic monotheistic religions as a man who was utterly present to God and God's people throughout his life.

So what were God's first words?

'Let there be …'

What clues are there for noticing things about God at the beginning of this story? That will depend on how we hear this story read, the tone of voice, and where emphasis is being placed. The voice of authority and power is the default one. Perhaps there are other possibilities?

'Let there be …'

Could this voice be affirming and permission-giving? Creation is being allowed to happen. It seems to be full of possibilities. Is there even a kind of delegating going on? The humans are given the task of tending and caring for creation. This God allows his human creation to exercise a great of choice and initiative and so is open to the risk that we can, and do, get things horribly wrong.

'Let there be …'

This could be the voice of a project manager. The work of creation certainly seems carefully planned and timed over six days. Surely all that is needed has been ordered ahead? Can we imagine God, with lists in hand:

- At the builder's yard (raw materials for creating), the engineering works ('God made the vault' v.4).
- With the environmental/ecological agencies ('Let the water under the sky be gathered to one place, and let dry ground appear' v.9, and 'God made the wild animals' v.25 etc.).
- At the farmers market ('Let the land produce livestock', vv.24–25).
- At the garden centre ('Let the land produce vegetation' v.11).
- At the biology laboratory ('male and female he created them' v.27).

'Let there be ...'

This may be the voice of playful imagination. Could 'let there be' be a thoughtful pause between actions as new possibilities are considered – which are endless, of course, for with God all things are possible? It could have a 'Hmm, what if?' ... 'I wonder?' ... or 'How about?' feel to it. What if God is simply wondering aloud what to create next? Can we imagine creation as God playfully improvising out of an inexhaustible imagination? The priest and scientist John Polkinghorne once observed, 'Creation has more the appearance of an improvisation than the performance of a predetermined script' (Tippett, 2005). As we shall see, this is certainly the feel of God's approach in the second creation story.

'Let there be ...'

Might this be the voice of God speaking today, as it was in the beginning?

What do we hear? What is the tone of his voice? What is his desire for us?

What is he still willing that this world becomes?

What is he still calling into being in new ways?

Day by day, the possibilities of this gift of life flows out of the endlessly affirming, permission-giving, playfully imaginative desire of God.

5

Where the Wild Things Are

Here there be monsters

God created the great sea monsters and every living creature that moves, of every kind, with which the waters swarm, and every winged bird of every kind. (Gen. 1.21)

I was writing this chapter just as news broke that the fossil of a colossal sea monster had been found in the cliffs of Dorset's Jurassic Coast. The Pliosaur terrorized the oceans about 150 million years ago. It grew up to 15 metres long. Its skull alone is 2 metres long and it had huge teeth and jaws with the strength to bite a car in half.

These are the same cliffs where, in 1811, Mary Anning unearthed the giant fossil of an unknown creature. It was the first of a succession of finds that excited, unsettled and challenged the devout, but biblically literalist, Christian imagination of nineteenth-century Britain (Taylor, 2024, chapter 1).

It is Day Five of creation. God is now moving on to creating living creatures. No sooner said than done. Sea, land and air are suddenly teeming and swarming with life. God shows no interest in organizing it at all. This is *wild* life. Domestic livestock, created separately, are mentioned in passing, but seem very outnumbered. What God chooses to create first is a surprise. What might you imagine he would consider to be his first priority? What he actually makes are giant sea monsters (v. 21)! The storyteller simply reports this without comment and moves on. Curiously, this detail goes mostly unremarked. But God has more to say about these monsters in the epic creation poem found at the end of the book of Job.

After the long account of Job's appalling sufferings and his exhaustive attempts to find an explanation for them, chapters 38 to 42 of Job contain God's magnificent and dramatic response to Job out of the storm. This poem is much longer and more detailed than either account in Genesis but is hardly ever discussed alongside them. It begins with an extended celebration of the first days of creation, from the song of the morning stars and the joyful shout of heaven as the foundations of the earth were laid, to the hawk on the wing and the mountain goat giving birth. 'Where were you when I was doing all this?' God asks Job (Job 38.4). The sheer scale of imagination in this creating is overwhelming. God now turns his focus to his creation of two creatures – Behemoth and Leviathan. In ancient Near-Eastern religion these were terrifying, semi-mythical monsters representing the uncontrollable, chaotic forces of anti-creation and anti-God. They personify the existential human fear of the random element in life, and the anxiety that this may all fall back into primordial chaos and non-being.

In some of the psalms, these chaos monsters are the arch-opponents of God's purposes. Psalm 74.14 celebrates the power of God in overcoming and crushing Leviathan. At the far end of time, the book of Revelation foretells a coming time when chaos, personified by 'the dragon' or 'serpent', will be finally overthrown (Rev. 20.2, 10).

Here in Job the mood is very different. Behemoth and Leviathan are what God created first, in the beginning. Nor was this an accident. 'Look at Behemoth which I made just like you,' he says to Job. 'It is the first of the great acts of God – only its maker can approach it' (Job 40.15, 19). God clearly takes a particular delight in them and boasts of them at length. 'I will not keep silent concerning its mighty strength or its splendid frame ... Who can stand before it?' (Job 41.11, 12). God teases Job about his comparative frailty before them. 'Can you draw out Leviathan with a fish hook ... Will you play with it as with a bird, or will you put it on a leash for your girls? Any hope of capturing it will be disappointed; were not even the gods overwhelmed at the sight of it?' (from Job 41.1–9). The psalmist picks up this playful tone:

What a wildly wonderful world, God!
You made it all ... the deep, wide sea,
Ships plow those waters,
and Leviathan, your pet dragon, romps in them.
(Ps. 104.26, The Message)

Not only is this a world in which God begins by making these wild and untameable creatures, he looks back on them as the best things he did. Though he clearly acts upon their destructiveness, limits their power and, on occasion, overthrows them, he does not choose to remove them. Rather, they are for celebrating as part of the original gift of creation. God does not want a tame world. In this sense, we are called to wildness as much as to order. We must hold this in tension.

This searching wisdom tale began with God boasting to Satan about Job (1.8). Now God is boasting to Job about the animals and reminding him of his place by teasing him. 'Job is thus de-centred. God turns the issue from justice in the universe (a human ideal) to order in the universe (a divine prerogative)' (Murphy, 2001, pp. 165-6).

The picture we have here is both dangerous and exciting. Order and chaos coexist in this world in a dynamic relationship. If chaos is never allowed to bring life to a final disintegration, nor is order allowed to impose a total predictability on it. It is the tension between these two apparently opposing forces that makes freely chosen and creative living possible. If God created a world totally ordered by his will, life would be a sterile, repetitive, mechanical existence. Equally, if everything were random and left to chance, life would have neither the security nor shape that gives it meaning and purpose.

The presence of chaos monsters does not mean God has abandoned this world to chance or has withdrawn his care from it (though it may feel like that at times). There is another possibility. What if God is to be found in the midst of the wild, where choices are most vital and hazardous and the possibilities are most real? What if this is God's way of calling us into life – attracting, enticing, tempting us to take risks and live more boldly? We need no reminding that this world is not 'safe'.

The good news is, nor is God. 'Aslan is not a tame lion,' says Mr Beaver in *The Lion, the Witch and the Wardrobe* (Lewis, 1950, p. 80). But all too easily religion becomes a succession of sophisticated attempts to tame the wildness of God.

What if we are *drawn* to chance rather than abandoned to it?

6

All Good

The goodness of God

And God saw that it was good. (Gen. 1.10)

At each stage of creation we read that God pauses to review what he has just brought into being. Each time he likes what he sees. He declares it 'good'. On the seventh and last time it was all *very* good.

Why does this need saying at all? Was the result ever in any doubt? Of course it is good! God made it. God is good and God does not make mistakes. Is the narrator suggesting God was daily carrying out final checks for faults or mistakes? (That might explain Adam and Eve though – they were created on a Friday afternoon, after all.)

'Good' can mean a variety of things. Perhaps God is appreciating a good job done, admiring the technical virtuosity, delighting in the choice of colour schemes, and in the exhilarating variety in it all? This cannot be 'good' versus anything else, for the simple reason that there is nothing else. There is nothing to compare it all with.

It is certainly not 'good' versus 'bad' – for there was no sin in that world yet.

The commonly made assumption is that good means perfect. But the story never says that. And what would be the point of a perfect world anyway? It is very difficult to imagine what there would be for Adam and Eve to do in a perfect creation, which is probably why, in so much religious art, they are just vaguely standing around surrounded by lions, lambs and trees impossibly heavy with ripe fruit. What need would there be for any exercise of dominion? Nothing would need subduing or controlling in a perfect world. What work would there be for a gardener in a perfect garden? There would surely be no weeding to do or dead leaves to rake?

Instead, the word the storyteller chooses, repeatedly and deliberately, is 'good'. Good is not the same as perfect. We are being told something very important. Rabbi Jonathan Sacks points out what an utterly startling faith claim this is to make in that ancient, historic context. That world was routinely experienced as terrifyingly uncontrollable, full of danger, plagues, evil forces, gods at war and chaotic powers. It had no meaning or purpose. Human life and death came and went as so much collateral damage. In this creation account, God's people are being told something very different. This creation is good! It is the gift of single divine will and good purpose. 'Creation in Genesis is not primarily about the power of God, but about the goodness of God, and the universe He made' (Sacks, 2009, p. 51).

In a group discussion around this story someone suggested 'good' might be understood in the sense of 'good *enough*'. 'Good enough' parenting was a theory that originated with the pioneering psychoanalyst and paediatrician Donald Winnicott. The 'good enough' parenting of a young child enables the establishing of the secure attachment that a child vitally needs and from which they may grow and flourish in their own life and calling. The phrase has been extended to other relationships. A good enough relationship is one that has created trust and gives security and confidence to both parties, and from which each may enter and explore the life that is theirs.

In other contexts, 'good enough' has a negative meaning, of course. It suggests something second-best, offered in a casual, half-hearted way. As it is used here, though, 'good enough' is a wholly positive affirmation. Good enough offers everything needed for the task required. The supreme quality of a good enough relationship is the gift of space. In a good enough relationship there is no clinging or possessing. It leaves the space to grow. It lets be. The root of the Hebrew word 'to be saved' means 'to make spacious'. A good enough world is a generously spacious one – as it was in the beginning. By contrast, perfection allows no such space or room to move at all. In a world of perfection we can only fail.

The God we meet in this creation story is a good enough God.

Jonathan Sacks tells of his visits to addiction centres, prisons and young offenders' institutions that was part of his work as Chief Rabbi. He noted how none of those he met there had wanted their lives to go that way. They would speak of lost hopes and ambitions. Life, and people, had let them down. The reasons were varied. Some grew up in dysfunctional homes without role models or anyone they could trust, or who was there for them. They had to find their way in life with little or no sense of their own worth or self-respect. They had stumbled through poor choices or lack of guidance. Sacks noted that there was a basic lack at the heart of their lives. 'No one ever told them that they were good.' He says that to see good in others and to tell them is 'one of the great creating acts'. 'When we recognise the goodness in someone, we do more than create it, we help it to become creative. This is what God does for us' (Sacks, 2009, p. 27).

In my experience, Christians often struggle to hear this affirmation or even think it is wrong. We find it much easier to assume God is telling us off – 'You are sinners' – and to believe we are *not* good enough. Have you ever heard God tell you – 'You are good'? Can you imagine God drawing near to you in love and joy and declaring, 'You are good.' Can you sense his delight at your creating? Try it. It is true.

This story tells us that what is original to this world is not chaos, evil or sin – but goodness. We can trust this. It is more than enough.

7

The First Bible

Creation as revelation

From the beginning, you have created all things
and all your works echo the silent music of your praise.
(*Common Worship*, p. 201)

'Where were you when I laid the foundation of the earth?', God abruptly demands of Job. The answer is 'nowhere' of course. None of us were in existence on that day 'When the morning stars sang together, and all the heavenly beings shouted for joy' (Job 38.7).

Creation has had its own life in God long before the first human footprints appeared on the surface of this earth. The era of the dinosaurs alone lasted over 150 million years and they only occupy a very small place in the story. To make this point the storyteller has compressed billions of years into a few brief days, the intention being to reveal the source of what is emerging. It is all the work of God. On the timeline of all this, humanity occupies a virtually invisible sliver of existence on the most recent edges of emerging life. We are part of something so unimaginably greater than ourselves. So, before we read of the appearance of humankind, we may do well to pause and reflect on the world in which we have so recently appeared.

The universe is the first act of divine revelation. For that reason, creation has been called the first Bible by Augustine, Aquinas and many others. That is not such a startling thought. For what other source of wisdom has humanity had for the greater part of our life on earth?

Creation is not in competition with the revealed Word. The claim does not imply biblical revelation is being usurped. It is a natural idea in scripture itself where St Paul writes that, 'Ever since the creation of the world his eternal power and divine nature, invisible though they are, have been understood and seen through the things he has made' (Rom. 1.20). The written word reveals what creation has always known.

'The world is charged with the grandeur of God,' wrote Gerard Manley Hopkins. 'It will flame out, like shining from shook foil;/ It gathers to a greatness ...'

In the psalms and elsewhere creation is to be found exuberantly engaged in the worship of God – mountains, seas, trees, animals and birds are praising and proclaiming for all they are worth:

> The heavens are telling the glory of God;
>   and the firmament proclaims his handiwork.
> Day to day pours forth speech,
> and night to night declares knowledge.
> There is no speech, nor are there words;
>   their voice is not heard;
> yet their voice goes out through all the earth,
>   and their words to the end of the world. (Ps. 19.1–4)

The Bible speaks of this endlessly proliferating creation as a work of divine wisdom (Ps. 104.24). We are only now becoming aware of just how amazingly intricate and vulnerably interdependent relationships are within the natural world: phenomena like the mycorrhizal network,[1] for example, popularly called the Wood Wide Web, reveal hidden patterns of diversity, mutuality and inclusion that enable the flourishing and growth of the whole.

The contemplative monk Thomas Merton urged attentive listening to the created world, even as it was being increasingly plundered for profit. In one memorable reflection, he tells of a time in his hermitage when a passing storm brought torrential

---

1 For a brief explanation, see https://www.nationalforests.org/blog/underground-mycorrhizal-network, accessed 14.07.2024.

rain. He was so absorbed by it his supper burned on the stove, unnoticed:

> I was listening to the rain. [It] surrounded the whole cabin [with] a whole world of meaning, of secrecy, of silence, of rumour. Think of it: all that speech pouring down, selling nothing, judging nobody, drenching the thick mulch of dead leaves, soaking the trees, filling the gullies of the wood with water! The rain reminds me again and again that the whole world runs by rhythms I have not yet learned to recognize. What a thing it is to sit in the forest, at night, cherished by this wonderful, unintelligible, perfectly innocent speech, the most comforting speech in the world, the talk that rain makes by itself. Nobody started it, nobody is going to stop it. It will talk as long as it wants, this rain. And as long as it talks, I am going to listen. (Merton, 1964, pp. 9–10)

There is, I think, another gift in our relationship with creation. One easily missed. I have written elsewhere of a time, some years ago, when I withdrew to an Alpine cabin on my own for some months (Runcorn, 1990, pp. 91ff). I had burned out and was quite broken. On one occasion I found myself weeping helplessly for a prolonged period of time. It left me feeling lost and frightened. As the tears dried, I knew a mixture of numbness and heightened awareness that can often follow an outpouring of grief. I became aware of the stove behind me, the wood crackling and clunking in it, while the leaky old kettle on top hissed and steamed. It had the feel of a close friend who watched and understood and kept silent company. The rough plank walls of my cabin felt supportive and sheltering, without closing in upon my space. I looked out of the window down the steep valley sides. The pasture grasses were rippling on the evening breeze. The clouds tugged at the mountain peaks. I felt the cooling air of the approaching night. Everything around me seemed to know and understand a secret that, simple though it was, still eluded me. All I knew was that in that moment I was held in what I have always called the companionship of creation.

Harry Williams made a similar connection. He was a profound writer on the business of faith and life, neither of which came easily to him. His life was often marked by periods of struggle and depression. He spoke of

> ... the sense of belonging to the natural world. The compelling conviction that, in spite of all the evidence to the contrary, in spite of all the suffering we may have to witness or to undergo, the universe is on our side, and works not for our destruction but for our fulfilment. (Williams, 1965, p. 118)

In its turn, St Paul says, creation is waiting 'with eager longing' for its freedom and 'groaning in labour pains' (Rom. 8.19–23) as it waits for the fulfilling of all things that will come in the renewing of heaven and earth.

> This music has been playing from the beginning.
> There are songs to learn, wisdom to listen to.
> This world is hidden sacrament waiting to be revealed.

8

Looking Like God

Being made in God's image

'*Let us make humankind in our image, according to our likeness.*' (Gen. 1.26)

In a local National Trust property, the walls in every room are covered with portraits of the family who once lived there. They trace a line that goes back several hundred years. One distinguishing feature makes their relationship to one another immediately recognizable. It is the family nose. Clothing and fashion vary widely but, generation to generation, that nose is there, even in the most recent family photos on the piano. Women and men together all bear the same likeness.

What does it mean to be told that our finite humanity bears the image and likeness of God – who is eternal, is spirit, all powerful, all knowing, and who we cannot see? Clearly, to be in God's image is not to share his being. That is impossible. So what is this 'likeness'? Where and how do we image God in our humanity?

The question has been argued over at great length down through church history, despite the fact that, once past this verse, the idea is barely mentioned again in the Bible until St Paul writes of Christ as the 'image of God' (2 Cor. 4.4).

To theologians in the early centuries this suggested a developmental model. 'Image' refers to our present, fallen, state. 'Likeness' refers to what we shall become in our final restored state. Double references like these are typically Hebrew ways of stressing a point. But there is no fallen state at all in the story at this point.

Augustine and others favoured the idea that our likeness

is found in our unique mental capacities, which distinguish humans from the animal world. A destructive legacy of this, though, has been the tendency to treat the mind as superior, and to despise our material world, and embodied life, as fallen. The Bible never does this. Humanity there is a rounded whole – mind, body and spirit.

A relatively recent theory locates the image and likeness of God in the union of male and female in marriage. This is more commonly to be found in biblically conservative circles and in some Roman Catholic teaching on marriage. By this understanding, the marriage union completes or re-unites humanity and thus becomes a unique reflection of God's image. Unsurprisingly, the view forms the basis for some approaches to debates about gender and same-sex relationships. The Bible text knows nothing of this idea, which also confuses the distinction between God's will for creation and God's own being, which is beyond gender and sexual identity. Furthermore, it wholly excludes from the image of God any other expressions of human living and relating outside marriage. Single people like St Paul would be excluded. Here in Genesis God creates *all* humanity in his image and likeness, not just some or particular categories of human belonging and relationships.

In the Middle Ages the rabbis agonized over this text. It was a complete contradiction to them. Do not the scriptures expressly forbid the making of images? How are we to be images of God without falling into the sin of idolatry? But this likeness is not a work of self-creation at all. We do not make ourselves like God. To be found in his likeness is his choice and gift.

So where and how do we image God? The rabbis approached the question this way: God utterly transcends nature. He can speak into nothing and create whatever he chooses. That endlessly creative freedom is surely what is core to such a God. To be made in the divine image, then, is to be capable of being freely, imaginatively creative. To be in God's likeness is to express our lives with creative choices and generous imagination. We are God's representatives and delegates, life-givers and creators after his image. They were surely right. Image and likeness are clearly linked to the verses that follow about the calling of human beings to the care of creation. To be made in God's image is to be creative and to share in the work of care for that which God has made.

Possibly the most obvious meaning of this verse is the most widely neglected one. When reading a text or passage of scripture an important question to ask is, 'What would this have meant to those to whom it was first spoken?' In that ancient world, kings were absolute rulers, demanding to be worshipped as semi-divine beings. They built large, imposing images of themselves, requiring sacrifice and veneration. Even today such images are features of more despotic regimes. Political or religious, those images were signs of oppression, hierarchy, dominance and subjugation. Here in Israel's scriptures, in the beginning, *all* humanity is made in God's image, from least to greatest, male and female, without condition. All are equal in the likeness of a God who does not oppress, has no interest in status or reputation, does not demand unquestioning allegiance, and who gives life to all. There is no mistaking how uniquely important the storyteller finds this moment in the creation narrative. God's forming of humanity in the divine image and likeness is repeated three times.

So here we find ourselves, declared to be in the image of a God we cannot see. The text is surely forward-looking. We must do the same, discovering as we go. 'Beloved,' wrote John, 'we are God's children now; what we will be has not yet been revealed. What we do know is this: when he is revealed, we will be like him, for we will see him as he is' (1 John 3.1–3). We are being invited to think in terms of the possibilities of things, rather than to go seeking definitions or to speculate over some fixed original state of being in ways the text knows nothing of. Imagine that.

9

Taking Care

Ecology, dominion and subduing the earth

Then God said, 'Let us make humankind in our image, according to our likeness; and let them have dominion over the fish of the sea, and over the birds of the air, and over the cattle, and over all the wild animals of the earth, and over every creeping thing that creeps upon the earth.' ... God blessed them, and God said to them, 'Be fruitful and multiply, and fill the earth and subdue it; and have dominion over the fish of the sea and over the birds of the air and over every living thing that moves upon the earth.' (Gen. 1.26, 28)

Scientists are presently locked in debate about whether to designate this stage of earth history 'Anthropocene'. The name is already widely in use. It is given to an era that is experiencing significant planetary change as a result of dominant human activity. This would include burning fossil fuels, deforestation, pollution and much besides. The age we are leaving is called 'Holocene', a largely settled era spanning nearly 12,000 years. One feature of the present age is the accelerating speed of change. For the first time in the history of the world one of its creatures has the collective capability to destroy itself and its own living environment.

Some lay the blame for this situation at the door of the Christian faith and the Bible. The language of 'dominion', 'filling' and 'subduing' in this creation story does appear to support this claim. It has certainly been heard at times as a divine mandate to dominate and exploit. In fact, the Old Testament reveals a very practical awareness of environmental responsibilities. Laws in the Bible governing farming and food production, for example, show an understanding of responsible land management as well as urging compassionate practices to ensure that the poor and the foreigners in our midst do not go hungry.

For a prolonged period of history, however, Christian faith was the official religion of western nations whose military, economic and imperial ambitions led directly to global exploitation and the plundering of the earth's natural resources without regard for sustainability. We are now much more sensitive to the challenges of managing the earth responsibly, but are continuing to struggle to agree and commit to what the task urgently requires. The storyteller interweaves the call to care for the earth with repeated references to humanity being in the image and likeness of God. Humankind's presence and work in the world is to reflect God's own character and ways.

Speaking of humankind's relation to earth in terms of 'have dominion over', to 'rule' and 'hold sway' are misleading, though, and do not express the original sense of the story being told. Ellen Davis prefers to translate these as 'exercise skilled mastery over' (2019, p. 55). Others note that the Hebrew word 'radah' does not in fact mean 'rule' in an authoritative sense. It is more a pastoral word and its meaning is better illustrated by the work of a shepherd wandering through the landscape caring for their flock of sheep. Furthermore, the Hebrew word for 'over' can also mean 'among'. Notice how this changes the tone and character of the original commission. 'Have dominion over' becomes 'exercise skilled mastery among'. The focus shifts away from an exercise of power over, to the skilled fulfilling of a particular task on behalf of. The work of stewardship is shared 'among' and expressed 'in the midst'. This finds common ground with some contemporary approaches to Christian leadership.

The command to 'subdue' is altogether more shocking though. That common translation significantly mutes what the storyteller actually says. In the Hebrew, God tells humankind to 'fill the earth and *conquer* it'. This seems to tip us straight back into the language of exploitation. The storyteller knows what he is doing, though. Perhaps he thought the shock was needed. For this is exactly what the people of Israel were commanded to do at the end of their wilderness wanderings – to enter the land of Canaan and conquer it. No ancient hearer would miss that connection. Here it is applied to the whole earth. But is 'conquering' any better than 'dominion' and 'subduing'? Is it surprising translations opt for something more – well – subdued?

We can only understand the storyteller's intention by re-entering the world of those first hearers, as best we can. They are being spoken to very provocatively through the use of that word 'subdued'. We have already noted how this story was first told among a people in exile. They were hearing God's command to exercise full stewardship of the earth from precisely the same situation as their ancestors in the wilderness. They are landless. Boldly connecting the conquest narratives of Canaan to the original vocation to steward the earth is a way of reminding Israel of their first calling. Both conquests were a call to represent divine will and purpose in a world that is God's, and in which he intends all to flourish and be blessed. 'Skilled mastery' is needed to lead the world into this. To those hearers in exile this text is so encouraging – their vocation, and God's original intention, is not revoked. It is also deeply challenging, for *both* conquests failed in their call to be stewards of the divine blessing and flourishing of the earth. They are hearing this in exile. They have, themselves, been conquered.

Before we move on from the discussion of these particular words and their meaning we need reminding that all the language of power in the Bible needs reading and interpreting with great care if it is not to do great harm. The continued unresolved tensions and suffering in that historic land is testimony to this.

What we are hearing in these verses are both encouragements and the challenges for the Anthropocene crisis of our own time. With the vocation to manage creation comes the exercise of enormous power and the need for even greater insight and responsibility. God is surely taking a huge risk! The question is how such active management is to be exercised. The commission to humanity is directly linked to our being made in God's image and likeness. The way we go about the task is to reflect God's own character and good purposes for all the world, and to be the means of his blessing to all.

The Anglican church has adopted something it calls 'The Five Marks of Mission' to summarize its understanding of its life and calling in the world. The fifth mark is 'to strive to safeguard the integrity of creation and sustain and renew the life of the Earth'. The 'Marks' are often shortened to five words: tell, teach, tend, transform and treasure. Our mission to creation is more than simply keeping it safe. We are to treasure it.

10

Sabbath Play

Creation complete in God

*And on the seventh day God finished the work that he had
done, and he rested on the seventh day from all the work that
he had done. So God blessed the seventh day and hallowed it,
because on it God rested from all the work that he had done
in creation.* (Gen. 2.1–3)

The outer walls of Chartres Cathedral, in France, are crowded
with sculptures of Bible stories and characters. There are
several of God and Adam. In one, Adam is standing behind
God, looking out over his shoulder. God's hand is outstretched
as if showing him something. The image is restful and companionable. They are enjoying surveying a new world together,
completed in God's goodness and inexhaustible imagination. It
is the sabbath.

It is day seven. God pronounces a special blessing on this day,
and no other. For what reason exactly? An incredible work has
come to its initial completion, made by a God who had no need
to create at all. What is there to do now? Either this project
is completely meaningless, or it is an invitation to play. In the
wisdom literature of the Bible creating is playful work. This
is not to trivialize it. Play can be a very serious activity. Jesus
complained his world was like children in the marketplace who
wouldn't dance or play (Matt. 11.17).

When the Bible was divided into chapters and verses in the
sixteenth century, the first chapter break in Genesis was on
the sixth day. This had the effect of leaving human beings at
the centre of the story. But the crowning point of creation is not
humankind. It is the sabbath. It is thought that setting aside such

a day, within regular structured time, was previously unknown in that ancient world. God's people were being called to live a new story. This is a matter of profound significance. Sabbath is what *God* does. We are made in his image. The sabbath is where we most fully realize our likeness to God. The sabbath is for delighting in God. Life is re-centred around worship. This was in total contrast with the religions of the surrounding nations, where humanity was created to be slaves of the gods. Now it is true that both Jews and Christians have been guilty of reducing the sabbath to a set of legalistic rules at times. It was a regular complaint of Jesus against the religious authorities of his day. 'The sabbath was made for humankind, and not humankind for the sabbath,' he said (Mark 2.27). God seeks a non-utilitarian relationship. We exist simply because God delights in us and desires our company.

Without a sabbath principle in our lives we are prey to all forms of oppression – including religious ones. We lose precisely the context that God gives us in which to know ourselves and celebrate life in him. In contemporary living, overwork is endemic with all the stresses and health issues that inevitably go with it. We lack the most essential boundaries, while magazines and newspapers endlessly offer hints and tips on better lifestyles, diet, sleeping better and switching off. The diagnosis does not go deep enough. We need regular expressions of what the ancient sabbath provided. Sabbath renews us in the truth of who we are and where we find our worth and identity. In this context, John Goldingay remembers his late wife Anne who had multiple sclerosis and in her last years could not move or speak at all. He describes her living 'in a perpetual sabbath', a reminder that being made in God's image is not for measuring in productivity and usefulness (Goldingay, 2010a, pp. 25–6).

For many, taking a whole day, as traditionally prescribed, is simply not possible. As with all we read in the Bible, our task is to discern the original intention of the text as best we can, and then seek how it might be faithfully applied in our contemporary context. Finding space for making sabbath in our lives is important. It is significant that in the Bible the first thing God calls holy (hallowed) is not a thing, place or person, but time itself. The sabbath day is far more than work/life balance. Rather, 'It invites us to forge a pattern of living in which work and creativity are complemented by rest and renewal' (Atwell, 2011, p. 33). I do not rest so that I can just get busy again. Rest and work form part of the whole gift of life in God, and sabbath time renews in us the wholeness of that gift.

Sabbath rest and play is subversive activity. It relativizes the powers, mocks authorities, and contradicts the scripts that drive us. Jean-Jacques Suurmond writes of the significance of the sabbath in the Pentecostal tradition, the fastest growing church in the world. Its communities are found among the poorest and most oppressed societies, with little choice over their time and activities. The sabbath, for them, is God's time, a playful subversion of the powers, a protest against false gods and injustice, and a joyful cry of liberation. Play has an 'as if' quality to it. So does the sabbath. It 'creates a free space in which God's purpose with the world becomes transparent. For a whole day people abandon their work in the belief that it is not their work, but only grace that can save them' (Suurmond, 1994, p. 32).

In a delightful passage in Proverbs, wisdom is described as God's master builder at the beginning of creation. As so often, the meaning is not completely clear and there are different ways of understanding the phrase, but the mood of these verses carries such an intense sense of delight – wisdom is having such fun! – that some translations opt for the image of a child playing with God and humanity in the workshop of this world.

> I was a child by his side.
> I was full of delight day by day,
> playing before him all the time,
> playing in his inhabited world
> and full of delight with humanity.
> (Prov. 8.30–31; Suurmond, 1994, p. 32)

This has led Suurmond to the suggestion that humans should not be called Homo sapiens (thinking/reasoning) but Homo *ludens* (play). For the theologian Raymond Brown this playful spirit includes our relationship with the Bible. 'After all, in the

Scriptures we are in our Father's house where the children are permitted to play' (Brueggemann, 2021, p. 402).

Finally, the sabbath looks forward. It offers a taste of the time when humankind and all creation finally rests complete and plays unhindered in the childlike wisdom of God.

11

The God Who Tells Stories

Reading the Bible

Storytelling is clearly God's favourite way of talking to us. It was for Jesus too. So it is not surprising that a people created in God's image should be found doing the same. When the people of Israel were wrestling with faith and understanding they told a story. Even the great sagas of 1 and 2 Samuel, or Exodus, are not history in the modern sense of the word. They are really a form of wisdom literature – extended theological reflections on history, as a people sought to learn from where they have come, sifting their stories for the signs of God in order to guide their faith in their own age.

To read and understand the Bible involves listening to stories originally told in very different languages, times and cultures from our own. The first discipline is to pay attention to the story that is actually being told, on its own terms. If we come to the Bible simply looking for answers to our questions and problems we will be in danger of only reading through the lens of our needs and anxieties.

In that respect, the creation stories are among the most mis-used and misunderstood parts of the Bible. Wonderfully subtle and nuanced storytelling has too often been assumed to be delivering explanations for the origins of sin, death and evil and more. It has been forced into the front line of battles for Christian orthodoxy that includes defending the faith against the most recent claims of science, evolution, biology or other 'liberal' tendencies.

Down through history, the church, with its Bible open, can be found initially resisting, and then come to critically integrate (to varying degrees), the emerging insights of cosmology, social sciences, medical research and much else. This has consistently required us to reconsider what kind of revelation the Bible actually is, the nature of its authority, and how it speaks into the fresh challenges and experiences each generation encounters. Scripture itself calls us to this journey. Many of the conflicts over what we claim 'the Bible says' centre around confusion as to how the Bible is saying it.

In the world of biblical studies there has been a move towards a greater focus on the importance of narrative and away from an over-emphasis on technical analysis of sources, words and texts. Jewish theologian and Bible translator Robert Alter believes that English translators too often fail to faithfully express the original text. One reason for this failing is what Alter calls the 'heresy of explanation'. Translators (and preachers) can be distracted with the need to make the Bible accessible instead of the primary task of representing it faithfully in another language (Alter, 1998, p. xv). The very aim of making the Bible easier to understand for modern readers can work against hearing what the Bible is actually saying. That is what led him to produce his own interpretation of the Hebrew Bible.

Alter observes how the biblical narratives make sophisticated use of language, including word play, punning, alliteration, poetry and complex literary structures. 'The storyteller delights in leaving the audience guessing about motives, and connections, and, above all, loves to set ambiguities of word choice and image against one another in an endless interplay resisting neat resolution' (Alter, 1998, p. xv). We are left wondering. And that is the whole intention, of course. The very strangeness of the text is part of its gift. We must not smooth it out.

Alter observes that all these literary methods are recognizable features in good fiction writing today. Now, speaking of the Bible text as storytelling, and making comparisons with modern fiction, may be rather alarming for some. Is not this God's revealed, inspired word? But belief in divine inspiration of the Bible is not undermined by this emphasis. God's inspiration is working precisely through the storyteller's faithful imagination and art, conveying what the Spirit of God is saying. The Israeli novelist Amos Oz points out that there was no word for 'fiction' in ancient Hebrew. Modern Hebrew had to create a word for it. That alerts us to the fact that the Bible does not distinguish between fact and fiction in the way we do. If you go looking for the novels of Jane Austen or J. K. Rowling in Tel Aviv central library, you will find them in the section called 'Narrative Prose'. Oz prefers this as a category of literature because 'fiction' commonly carries the suspicion of something that is not true, made up. In fact, fiction, in literature, has always been a way of exploring truth. Furthermore, not all that claims to be 'fact' is actually true. We are now much more aware, for example, of how often national histories, claiming to be factual records, contain biased and prejudiced reporting of events. By contrast, historical fiction can be a profound reflection on actual events and their meaning (Guppy, 1996).

'The Bible is very clear on this ...' is a claim that needs great care. Not because we lack confidence in it as God's word, but because belief in the divine inspiration of scripture does not override the discipline of paying careful attention to the *way* it is written. Reading the Bible is a work of interpretation. It involves far more than seeking a literal translation. Bible translator Eugene Peterson is clear that, 'The literal is almost always a bad translation – you can't get one language into another by being literal. Interpretation is always involved' (Collier, 2021, p. 242) The challenge is to get the tone and meaning of the original. We are seeking the 'spirit, the vibrancy of the text, the livingness of the message. The task is not to get back to the original but to re-create in the present' (Collier, 2021, p. 242).

The Bible is most truly reverenced, its authority honoured, its wisdom heard, its truth received, when the literary genre it has chosen to use is discerned and respected to the best of our ability and learning. When reading the creation narratives, that means listening to storytellers. They have important things to tell us.

12

One Creation – Two Stories

The Bible as conversation

The Bible begins with the creation of the world. That much we might expect.

But it does so by telling two very different stories of that work of creation, without offering any explanation. They have core convictions in common. In both, God is the sole creator and life-giver. In both, creation unfolds out of divine intention and purpose and is known, and flourishes, only in obedience and faithfulness to that intent. But thereafter, they contrast and even contradict each other.

In the first story, human beings are created last and are the crowning highpoint of creation and given dominion over what God has made. In the second story, Adam is created first, before anything else, in an empty world. In the first story, humans are created in the image of God. In the second story, Adam is created out of the dust of the earth. There is no mention of divine image. In the first story, creation happens over time. In the second, it happens in an instant. Creation proceeds to an ordered completion in the first. In the second story, it is unfinished, continuing, and even appears to be experimental. The first creation is repeatedly declared good. In the second, creation is *not* good for the first human. To sort out that problem God creates a myriad of creatures for him, none of which fulfil what Adam needs. So finally, by special action, God creates a human partner for him, the woman. The first creating is entirely by divine decree. In the second, though, God leaves significant parts of it to the choice of Adam. God the creator takes on a serving role to assist the human in his needs.

As noted in the last chapter, discerning what the Bible says first requires us to carefully attend to how it says it. We learn from these first pages that the Bible does not choose to speak or teach with one voice. That should not be a complete surprise. After all, the New Testament starts with four versions of the same gospel. But it is unsettling if we feel that this suggests that our authoritative guide to life and faith is unclear or even contradicts itself. Faced with two very different creation stories at the beginning of the Bible, the most common response is to attempt to forcibly harmonize the two versions. But contrasting stories they clearly are. So we must assume they are meant to be so. Rather than try and blend them into one we must learn to let them talk to each other.

Here are four ways of expressing the way the scriptures speak with more than one voice.

Music

Theological writer and teacher Ellen Davis likes the word 'polyphony'. This is a musical term meaning 'many sounds'. Polyphony consists of two or more lines of independent melody, playing simultaneously, as opposed to music harmonized around one tune. In literature, polyphony describes narrative which includes a diversity of simultaneous points of view and voices. This is a technique that is popular among modern novelists. For Davis, polyphony describes the scriptures where 'most of the books were composed and shaped by multiple writers and editors, and so have no single voice or point of view' (Davis, 2019, pp. 5 and 17).

Montage

A montage (literally: 'putting together') is a film sequence technique made up of many short scenes, edited together. They contrast with one another and are not harmonized. Taken together they form part of a bigger picture in which the wider narrative emerges. Bible translator and commentator Robert Alter suggests that scripture narratives include such multiple perspectives, not smoothed out into a single utterance, but offering 'a montage of viewpoints arranged in sequence' (Alter, 2011, pp. 141–53).

Theatre

The Old Testament theologian John Goldingay observes how the Bible more often 'shows' rather than 'tells'. It leaves things open rather than explains. It presents rather than expounds or declares (Goldingay, 2000, p. 132). Reading scripture like this becomes an experience rather like open theatre within which we, the audience, have a part to play in the unfolding drama. In this play, the church and world today are the act before the final one, when God will bring the story to completion. Until then we engage with all the voices before us as we seek to discern what the texts teach and how they can best guide us for life and faith today.

Conversation

The medieval theologian Erasmus translated the Bible from Greek into Latin. The challenge he continually faced was how to express a message, written in Greek, in terms Latin readers would relate to. In the opening verse of his gospel John chose the Greek word 'Logos' to express what was 'in the beginning'. English versions translate this 'the Word'. However, 'Logos' means much more than just a word or statement. It expresses something more like the whole creative principle of life. Erasmus, and the early Latin translators, struggled with the inadequacy of any single word to convey the meaning of Logos to express the truth and meaning of Christ. Erasmus did not translate Logos with the usual 'verbum' – the Latin meaning 'word'. He avoided it because he wanted to express something less directive. Apart from anything else, he was clear that people do not learn by simply being told what to believe. Something more dynamic, interactive and alive was needed. He chose 'sermo', meaning discourse. So, his translation of John's Gospel starts, 'In the beginning was the conversation.'

In fact, a dialogical approach has always been the way the church has sought a faithful and discerning reading of scripture (Runcorn, 2020, chapter 3). With the Bible open, understanding and meaning is never exhausted as the theological conversation continues, engaging the questions posed by life and faith within each new generation.

In the beginning was the conversation – and it continues today.

13

The Dust Creature

The first human

Then the Lord God formed man from the dust of the ground, and breathed into his nostrils the breath of life; and the man became a living being. (Gen. 2.7)

God is playing in the mud. In my happiest childhood memories, I am doing just that. 'Look what I have made!' In the first creation account God created by decree, from a lofty, sovereign distance. Here, we find God hands-on, down in the dirt of a lifeless, damp, pre-world flood-plain, 'crafting'.

After the ordered precision of the first storyteller, this account begins with a long rambling, single sentence:

> In the day that the Lord God made the earth and the heavens, when no plant of the field was yet in the earth and no herb of the field had yet sprung up – for the Lord God had not caused it to rain upon the earth, and there was no one to till the ground; but a stream would rise from the earth, and water the whole face of the ground – then the Lord God formed man from the dust of the ground, and breathed into his nostrils the breath of life; and the man became a living being. (Gen. 2.4–7)

The mud model complete, God leans over it and blows life into its nostrils. That is a gift of the most personal and intimate kind. If you are close to someone's breath, you are close to their very being. What is crafted is both from the dust of the earth and the breath of God. This is one creating act. We should only speak of body and soul here if we are clear we are speaking of one whole being, fully alive. I find imagining that moment one of the most helpful ways of re-centring myself when trying to pray. I imagine God bending down over me. I lift my nostrils and breathe in deeply, as he breathes upon me. I receive my life afresh from God, as it was in the beginning.

Before the story's end, however, the same dust of the ground is being spoken of in a very different way.

'By the sweat of your face
    you shall eat bread
until you return to the ground,
    for out of it you were taken;
you are dust,
    and to dust you shall return.' (Gen. 3.19)

'Remember you are dust' are words that are spoken at the annual Ash Wednesday service. It marks the beginning of the ancient season of Lent, with its call to self-examination and penitence. There is a powerfully symbolic moment as the faithful are firmly marked on the forehead with a mixture of dust and ashes: 'Remember you are dust and to dust you shall return, repent and believe the gospel.'

What are we to remember under this sign of dust?

First, that we are mortal and finite. We have a beginning and we will have an end. What began as dust will return to dust. The first creation story spoke into the lives of a people in crisis, lost in a far country. The second is speaking with sharp spiritual insight into the Solomonic court of Israel in the tenth century BC. That era was the high point of Israel's nationhood – leadership, economy, military, philosophy, culture and the arts, and international influence. If the first story spoke to emptiness and failure, the second addresses fullness and success. The first speaks hope and a future to those living in a world of chaos and loss. The second is perhaps a commentary and warning on the first. It is saying, 'These are the challenges and perils that you face as you seek to be faithful to this human vocation.' The story warns against hubris and the presumptions of success and status. You think you are important and great? Go back to your beginnings. Remember you are dust.

Dust and ashes are ancient expressions of humbling, repentance, of acknowledged wrong. We fall. We are sinners. It may be that the root of sin is simply the refusal to live under this sign of dust. We are never in more peril than when we neglect or resist this truth about who we are. Does our perennial frailty and waywardness surprise God? It seems not. 'He knows how we were made; he remembers that we are dust' (Ps. 103.14). He must know what he is about.

Dust is not for despising. It is a source of wonder. The ancient storyteller could not have known what modern science reveals. The dust out of which this world is formed is a gift of the entire universe. The very substance of our being, the oxygen in our lungs, carbon in our muscles, calcium in our bones, iron in our blood, was all forged out of nuclear reactions and supernova explosions of stars long before the earth had come into being. The process continues. 'The cosmos is within us,' wrote astronomer Carl Sagan. 'We are made of star-stuff. We are a way for the universe to know itself.' Who can make anything of dust? God does. Dust is the core ingredient for his creating work. Furthermore, with the advances in DNA and scientific analysis a tiny handful of dust is all that is needed now to reveal the life and stories of our human past and world in amazing detail. The dust remembers us.

In the Ash Wednesday service, the call to remember our dustiness is followed by an invitation – 'repent and believe the gospel'. The creation story is being re-crafted. There is a gift to receive. Through the love of Christ, we begin again. We are still dust. God is still life-making. Somewhere in all this, God is still playing in the dirt and breathing his life into his creation.

Dust we are. But *desired* dust. Dust with a destiny. Like Adam.

14

The Garden

The making of Paradise

The Lord God planted a garden in Eden, in the east; and there he put the man whom he had formed. Out of the ground the Lord God made to grow every tree that is pleasant to the sight and good for food. (Gen. 2.8–9)

Comedian Victoria Wood once suggested that 'church is what people used to do on Sundays before God invented garden centres'. But God's love of gardens goes back to the very beginning.

In the story so far, God, the artisan, has just crafted the first human out of the mud of the empty flood plain, and brought it to life through the gift of his own breath. In the continuing story God is now a landowner, who plants a garden of exceptional abundance and beauty on his estate in Eden, to give work for his new creation, Adam.

The story pauses for a brief aside. The narrator adopts a change of voice for this too. Imagine a tourist bus has drawn up beside the garden of Eden. We find ourselves eavesdropping on the tour guide in full flow. The information on offer is factual and precise:

A river flows out of Eden to water the garden, and from there it divides and becomes four branches. The name of the first is Pishon; it is the one that flows around the whole land of Havilah, where there is gold; and the gold of that land is good; bdellium and onyx stone are there. The name of the second river is Gihon; it is the one that flows around the whole land of Cush. The name of the third river is Tigris, which flows east of Assyria. And the fourth river is the Euphrates. (Gen. 2.10–14)

The tour party moves on and out of earshot.

Precise place names and geographical details like these easily give the impression that this must be a 'true story' set in an actual time and place in history. But it is not quite so straightforward. In the first place, not all that information is factually or geographically accurate. Eden was a region located in Mesopotamia, modern-day Iraq, some distance to the east of Israel. The focus on the rivers is a natural one. The climate of that region was harsh. Water is essential for life, and water there is, in abundance, around and across Eden. The Tigris and Euphrates were significant rivers in the Mesopotamian region. But Gihon is actually a spring, not a river – a source of water for Jerusalem. It does not, therefore, flow all 'round the whole land of Cush' (modern-day Ethiopia). Pishon is unknown today, though some ancient authorities thought it was the Nile. Egypt is one of several places where the Havilah is thought to be located. The truth is that we do not know. Places change their names and rivers change their flow. More to the point, however, these rivers do not all flow out of one geographical source in Eden.

What are we to make of all this? Perhaps this is the equivalent of the errors and omissions found on very early medieval maps of the world? The guide is being as accurate as the current knowledge available.

When read as poetry, though, this shows Eden as the theological source of all life, flowing out into all creation, and sustaining it all. This is a theological story. The focus is on God and what he is about. It always is.

Geography serves theology in this story. The narrator is not attempting to write a Lonely Planet guide for the ancient Near East. When the first hearers were told that Eden was 'to the east' (and a long way to the east if they were in Israel), was this the narrator's way of re-locating the imagination of his listeners? Stories often do their work like that. 'In a country far away, there was once a king who built a garden.' The legendary television series *Star Trek* was a brilliant contemporary example of this. Set in a far distant corner of the universe where 'no man had gone before', seeking out strange new planets and alien civilizations, each episode was a device for dramatically playing out significant contemporary questions and tensions in American society – race, war, religion, moral questions and relationships.[1]

Paradise gardens were artificial constructs. Eden means 'luxury' or 'delight'. Those ancient gardens of delight were a dramatic imagining of what life is meant to be, lived in the fullness of God's presence and gift – and perhaps the hope it may yet be so. They were places of hospitality, refreshment, rest, shelter, communion with God – a reminder of paradise. The word 'paradise' derives from a Farsi word meaning 'walled garden'. Everything essential for life to flourish was found there. It was a taste of heaven on earth.

In ancient Mesopotamia, the rulers and the wealthy would build 'gardens of delight'. The Hanging Gardens of Babylon are the most famous, though little is actually known about them. Cyrus the Great created a paradise garden round the sides of his palace. These gardens often covered wide areas and followed very particular designs, with themed sections. They contained ornamental and fruit trees, meadows, water features, pavilions and shrines. They were a delight to look at, laden with nourishing fruit and providing shade from the heat in the extreme temperatures of the Mesopotamian region. This garden tradition also has huge significance in the world of Islam, and over the centuries has influenced landscape design around the world. Smaller expressions of them can be found in the UK on historic estates and National Trust properties.

The scene is set for the telling of a story of such profound imagination that, in churches and beyond, it has occupied a central place in human faith and understanding throughout history.

---

1 The most famous example is the episode in 1968 widely remembered as showing the first-ever interracial kiss on American television. This came just a year after the American Supreme Court had declared mixed race marriage legal.

15

The Two Trees

Meaning and purpose

*Out of the ground the Lord God made to grow every tree that
is pleasant to the sight and good for food, the tree of life also
in the midst of the garden, and the tree of the knowledge of
good and evil.* (Gen. 2.9)

When my children were very young they were given a Bible picture book. The first illustration was the garden of Eden (the first
Genesis story was ignored). In the garden the sun is shining.
Flowers are in bloom everywhere. The scene is crowded with
every kind of species. Lambs lie curled up next to leopards. The
trees are in permanent harvest, groaning with luscious fruit.
Birds are singing. Adam and Eve are found in the midst of all
this, and although the story tells us they were not ashamed of
being naked, Eve's hair is very long indeed and the artist posi-
tions Adam behind a shrub with unusually wide leaves. They
are standing around looking vaguely happy, but with nothing to
do. The picture was the artist's sterile imagining of a non-exist-
ent world. My sons quickly went looking for more excitement.

This story of the garden of Eden is commonly read as a before-
and-after tale. Before – when creation was all wonderful and
perfect. After – when sin has happened, it has all gone horribly
wrong, and humanity is exiled from God and the garden. There
are two difficulties with this. First, we need to ask what that
tree is doing in the centre of the garden: the Tree of the Knowledge of Good and Evil. Why was there any need for such a tree
in a perfect creation? Where does the idea of evil even come
from in that world of original goodness? Second, there was no

'before' in any meaningful sense. Neither creation story spends any time attempting speculative descriptions of what perfect life was like before it all went wrong. Nor should we. That is not where the focus of this story lies.

Let's start again.

In the centre of the paradise garden of generous abundance and overwhelming fruitfulness, two particular trees are singled out for mention. The Tree of Life and the Tree of the Knowledge of Good and Evil. Every other fruit is on offer to the humans with an unrestricted eating policy. But eating from the Tree of the Knowledge of Good and Evil is forbidden. It will result in death. The storyteller plainly thinks no further explanation is needed. But that sudden, terse, prohibition changes the mood in paradise quite sharply for most of us.

In the Bible, trees are symbols of wisdom and metaphors for the character of, and blessing upon, a godly and devout life. They are mentioned frequently. 'A gentle tongue is a tree of life' (Prov. 15.4); 'The fruit of the righteous is a tree of life, but violence takes lives away' (Prov. 11.30); 'Desire fulfilled is a tree of life' (Prov. 13.12). Trees are a metaphor for life rooted securely in the way of wisdom:

> Happy are those
> who do not follow the advice of the wicked,
> but their delight is in the law of the Lord,
> They are like trees
> planted by streams of water,
> which yield their fruit in its season,
> and their leaves do not wither.
> In all that they do, they prosper. (Ps. 1.1–3)

The Tree of Life at the centre of God's garden makes sense. In another story it might be a spring or fountain. It locates the source of it all. Metaphorically, that tree is at the heart of all life that is faithfully rooted in God.

The Tree of the Knowledge of Good and Evil needs more unpacking – particularly the severe warning attached to it. It is found nowhere else in the Bible, so we have nothing to compare it with. If this tree was necessary, why were Adam and Eve forbidden from eating from it? Surely this is knowledge they need? What responsible and productive life is possible without the discernment of good and evil? The story gives no clue how they were supposed to obtain this knowledge.

The presence of that tree tells us this is a world of choices and possibilities, and therefore with significant consequences. Though the usual focus is on what is called 'Original Sin', this tree tells us creation was a place of Original Freedom. Without that tree in the garden there would be no story to follow of any interest or meaning. In a world of such generous, permissive freedom, the tree lays down boundaries. When boundaries and prohibitions are doing their proper job, they are not there to restrict, confine or to deny us life. They are there to guard our freedom.

It makes no sense to assume from this that God wants a world in which humans have no knowledge of good and evil. They would be dangerously naive and be no practical use to anyone. Nor does the story say that. The tree is there in the garden. We may assume it is doing its work. The wisdom life needs is present and provided for. The mistake was to assume that eating from that tree is what is needed. God clearly says it is not. In fact, it is dangerous to do so.

In the Bible wisdom begins when God is rightly feared. Not a cringing fear before a possessive God, but the honouring of God, what is his, and the way things are. Wisdom is God's alone to give, not ours to take. To ignore this is to attempt to be like God. It is a fatal mistake to try. The tree is a good and wise provision, telling us something we absolutely need to know. It is there to protect us. Our very lives depend on it. The way to know the difference between good and bad is to reverence God, honour and follow his ways.

That was the way of wisdom in the garden.

It still is.

16

Not Good to be Alone

The creation of the woman

Then the Lord God said, 'It is not good that the man should be alone; I will make him a helper as his partner.' So out of the ground the Lord God formed every animal of the field and every bird of the air, and brought them to the man to see what he would call them; and whatever the man called each living creature, that was its name. The man gave names to all cattle, and to the birds of the air, and to every animal of the field; but for the man there was not found a helper as his partner. So the Lord God caused a deep sleep to fall upon the man, and he slept; then he took one of his ribs and closed up its place with flesh. And the rib that the Lord God had taken from the man he made into a woman and brought her to the man. (Gen. 2.18–22)

One day, before anything yet existed on earth, God was walking on the damp, empty flood plains. He bent down and crafted a shape in the mud. God moved in very close, breathed into it, and gave it life. So it was that from the *adamah* (earth) the first *adam* (earth creature) emerged.

In the first account, creation was carefully ordered. This story, by contrast, has the feel of a folk tale in which God seems to be experimenting and spontaneously responding to emerging needs as they arise.

God has made the first human in a completely empty world. Adam has nowhere to live and nothing to do. So, God creates a garden and installs the human as the gardener. This may have always been the plan, but the feel is more spontaneous.

God suddenly declares, 'It is not good that the man should be alone; I will make him a helper as his partner.' What led to this pronouncement we are not told. But in that paradise garden, one thing is *not* good. The human is alone. It is no one's fault. Sin has not yet entered the world. This is life that is growing and developing in awareness. Even God is pictured as part of that. Incompleteness is one of the original good gifts in this world.

What God thinks Adam actually needs is much debated but two things are for clarifying. Being alone is not the same as being lonely. Adam, the gardener, was alone. Was the job proving too much for one person? Working alone is generally not a good thing. Either way, at this point in the story, Adam is seeking a suitable work colleague, not looking for love. Second, Adam is not gendered. In fact, it is not completely clear when the name 'Adam' moves from meaning 'humankind' to Adam, the male. But the story is not yet at that point.

God cannot meet the human's need. Instead, he assists him in the search. God improvises again, creating a huge variety of creatures and bringing them to Adam 'to see what he would call them' (Gen. 2.19). Naming and being named is central to knowing who we are and what story we are part of. God delegates this task to Adam. All are duly named but in none does Adam discern a 'help meet for him' (KJV).

God now takes the initiative. God creates an *'ezer kegedo'* for Adam, commonly translated 'helper' or 'helpmate'. But this easily suggests a secondary, supporting role – and indeed some believe it means precisely that. Since in the first story what was most important was created last, it is rather perverse though to suggest the one created second here is the lesser. Elsewhere in the Bible an *ezer* is someone who actively intervenes on behalf of another. 'More literally it suggests someone who is in front of you, or in sight of you, or opposite you' (Goldingay, 2010a, p. 39). An *ezer* therefore leads, has initiative, takes your side. This is not a relationship with any hierarchy. It is a partnership of mutuality and equality.

Adam must be put to sleep for this task. Why? We are not told. But in the Bible God does not usually allow humans to look on him directly or witness him at work. Moses must turn his back as God passes (Ex. 33.12–23). The resurrection too happens out of sight, in the dark. The world awakes to discover that something decisive has happened in the night. So it is with Adam. God forms a suitable companion out of Adam's rib. The word suggests skilled design. She is a work of art! She is brought to him when he wakes up and he greets her with utter joy.

'This at last is bone of my bones
    and flesh of my flesh;
this one shall be called Woman,
    for out of Man this one was taken.' (Gen. 2.23)

There is instant recognition. The job interview is forgotten. This is love. A story of a search for a working partner has merged into love and companionship.

This story has its roots in the assumptions of an ancient patriarchal culture but it also subverts them to a degree. The woman has been created entirely to meet the need of the man. She has no choice in the matter. She is allowed no reciprocal response to Adam's cry of joy. Adam, for all his delight in her, names her as he has named all the other animals – in this case, woman. But she is presented in a way that implies initiative, authority and mutuality.

In the first creation, God decreed everything. Here in the garden God decrees nothing (except what is *not* good). He takes a serving role. Only the human can recognize who they need as their partner. Adam must choose. Even when God creates the woman from *within* and *out of* Adam, the response is still his to make. So it is that humanity's first words on the face of the earth are of delight in mutual relationship. 'This at last is bone of my bones, and flesh of my flesh' (Gen. 2.23). 'There is no divine blueprint,' writes Garth Moore, 'there is only what makes glad the heart of each of us. The companionship which is in view in this text, is somebody you actually want to be with and share your life with. An imposed companion would be no companion at all' (Moore, 2003, p. 147).

17

Flesh of my Flesh

Human relationships

Therefore a man leaves his father and his mother and clings to his wife. (Gen. 2.24)

In the last chapter we followed the creation of a companion/ partner for the first human – woman. There is one further aspect of the story to consider. In debates about human sexuality and relationships this story has assumed a very central importance. Here in the garden, the claim is made, God definitively reveals his founding intention for humanity. It is marriage, between a man and a woman. Well, it was certainly a man and a woman in the beginning. Genesis 2, it is asserted, is a 'definition of marriage'. 'A gift of God in creation' is how the marriage service expresses it.

Now in a story telling of the origins of the human race that is a practical necessity! It would be very short story otherwise. And certainly, the loving partnership of male and female that enables the wonder of biological life creation is to be utterly honoured. No one is disputing that. But thereafter interpreting this story is not so straightforward.

Adam and Eve do not actually marry at any point in this story. The word itself does not even appear, though from the storyteller's passing comment we learn that his listeners inhabit a world where marriages happen (Gen. 2.24). The couple provide no illustration of what marriage looks like in practice. The storyteller's description of marriage as a leaving and cleaving is profound, but he did not get this from Adam and Eve. They had no home or family to leave! They are gendered but there is no interest in differences or roles – though Adam's delight in the woman is in their *similarity*, not difference. More surprising still, given the traditional focus on procreation in marriage, there is no family life in Eden. No children play among the trees in the cool in the evening. Sexual relations and childbirth only happen after the exile from the garden. No one has yet drawn any conclusions from the fact that children only appear in the story after the Fall!

Their actual relationship is not completely clear, though there are clues in the names. Hebrew storytelling loves puns. 'Adam' is a pun. Adam comes from the Adamah, the earth creature from the earth, the human from humus. And for most of the story that follows the Hebrew just speaks of *The* Adam – '*The* Human'. As already noted, the woman is named as a creature. Her response is not invited – 'I do'. She is given no choice or voice. And what might she have said? 'Well. Gosh. This is so sudden! I need more time. I don't even know your name.' Which is not surprising because The Human doesn't know his own name either at this point in the story! Neither of them receives a personal name until after 'The Fall'. 'The Adam' calls the woman Eve, 'mother of all', when she conceives their first child (Gen. 4.1). She is only called 'wife' when they are hiding from God in the bushes after eating from the forbidden tree (Gen. 3.8). 'The Adam' does not become a personal name for the man – Adam – until some years later, when their third child is conceived (Gen. 4.25). There are no definitions here. Rather, there is a subtle, evolving understanding of human personhood and identity is emerging.

How we interpret all this depends on what kind of story we think is being told. Is it prescriptive – laying down authoritative, divinely ordained, unchanging principles for all humanity for all time? It simply does not read like that. So much is left open and undefined. Adam and Eve's relationship is imprecise at least. Furthermore, no other relationships of any kind are found in the garden – children, family, friends and community. The couple are totally alone. How does this offer a guiding model for married life?

Finally, if this is a defining Bible statement of marriage, why were so few marriages in the Old Testament actually marriage?

Jacob, for example, committing adultery when he married Rachel while Leah was still alive (Gen. 29)? And what of the many wives, concubines and female slaves of Abraham, David and Solomon? All without censure. What of the legislation in the Torah permitting a man to take a second wife as long as he doesn't neglect the first one (Ex. 21.10)?

Marriage is certainly part of our beginnings, but it is not the main point being made here. To insist this is so is to make a category error. This story is descriptive, not definitive. Here is a wisdom tale inviting us into a divinely imagined world at its very beginnings, in which some core principles for human relationships are emerging and being tested through the first stages of the life of this couple.

There are four particular principles.

Human relationships are founded on recognition and choice

In the first creation story God decrees all that shall be in creation. Here in the garden God acts as a servant to Adam in his search. Only the human can choose who will fulfil their needs. And here contemporary Christian practice finds resonance with the ancient text. It is the couple who make a marriage, not the church. The couple minister the sacramental covenant of marriage to each other. The church witnesses and blesses what has *already been chosen*. That is why the service was formerly called the solemnization of holy matrimony. It is a public confirmation of something already in existence.

Human love is a leaving and cleaving

The word 'cleaving' is more often translated 'cling'. What this involves in the narrator's culture we are not told. But it is most movingly illustrated in the story of Ruth and Naomi. Life has been very hard for Naomi; having gone into exile to escape famine, she has lost her husband and both her sons. Depressed and embittered, she is returning from a far country to her hometown and her Hebrew people. She tells her Moabite daughter-in-law, Ruth, to leave her. Ruth refuses. She 'clings' to Naomi saying:

'Where you go, I will go;
    where you lodge, I will lodge;
your people shall be my people,
    and your God my God.' (Ruth 1.14–16)

The word 'cling' is the same one used in Genesis 2.24. That is surely deliberate, though Ruth's clinging is not sexual or marriage. It expresses something at the heart of all human commitment. Like many couples, my wife and I chose those verses for our wedding day. They said everything we wanted to say to each other in that moment. The same words, but from a very different relationship context and story, were guiding our understanding of marriage.

'Becoming one flesh'

This is commonly assumed to be a metaphor for love-making, and it certainly offers an apt poetic expression of the gift and significance of that sexual relationship. But in the Bible 'one flesh' does not mean sexual love. It actually means 'one kinship group' (see Gen. 29.14 and 1 Sam. 5.1). 'One flesh' is emphasizing the important place of marriage in the reshaping and renewing of primary kinship groups in society. Marriage is always part of a much bigger story of belonging.

Humanity is revealed in relationship

Recognition, choice, cleaving, community kinship and the care of creation are revealed as the life they are called to. The rest is left remarkably open. What other expressions of relationship, and marriage, and who may be part of them, are for each generation to explore. While we are unwilling to do this, we will be unable to respond faithfully to what this emerging world calls us to. But if we narrow this down to a story about one exclusive relationship, you exclude everyone else.

18

Called by Names

The changing names of God and the humans

As life emerges in the creation story, the names for God and for the humans keep changing. The narrator wants us to notice this, but it is easily missed in the English translations.

In the first creation story the name used for God is '*Elohim*'. 'In the beginning, Elohim created the heavens and the earth' (Gen. 1—2.4). Though Elohim speaks and is personally engaged in the work of creating, this ancient title is perhaps more of a collective noun than a name. Elohim is the force of nature, totality of all powers. Elohim is creator and judge, ordering all things so they have their place. Humankind is made in the image of Elohim, but they are not yet personally named or introduced any further either.

In the second account the name changes, or rather another name is added on. God is now the LORD God – in the Hebrew, *Yahweh Elohim*. (When English Bibles print LORD in capital letters, it is the divine name, Yahweh.) By partnering the name Yahweh to Elohim, the telling of the creation of the world becomes linked to the historic faith story of the people of Israel. Yahweh is the name revealed to Moses out of the burning bush, when Moses was being called to lead his people out of slavery in Egypt. Yahweh means 'I AM' or 'I am who I am'. Yahweh tells Moses, 'I have observed the misery of my people; I have heard their cry. I know their sufferings, and I have come down to deliver.' Yahweh is one who sees, hears, knows, cares and saves (Ex. 3.7–8). The revelation of God is unfolding.

A corresponding emergence, through naming, happens with

the human creation. In the first story, Elohim declares, 'Let us make humankind [Adam] in our image ... male [Hebrew: *Ish*] and female [*Ish-ah*] he created them' (Gen. 1.26–27). Male and female are named in the same way that other specific pairings of creation are named. Light and dark, land and water, are not opposite states though. They express the whole span of creation between. Likewise, 'male and female' is a way of saying 'all humanity'. The text does not say male *or* female and therefore makes no contribution to debates about human gender or marriage.

The names of the humans change too, as we saw in the last chapter. To try to highlight how subtly the storyteller uses names I am going to call Adam *The Human*, as the Hebrew does, because the English use of 'man' misleads. This is not yet the personal name of an individual, gendered male. It is not completely clear whether, when 'Adam' occurs in the Bible text, it means 'all humanity', or a gendered man, or is someone's personal name.

The Human is incomplete in some significant way. 'It is not good for The Human to be alone,' says Yahweh Elohim. 'I will make a helper suitable for him' (Gen. 2.18ff). We might ask if Yahweh Elohim really did not anticipate this would be the case? Nor are we told what exactly The Human was thought to be lacking. The scene that follows is actually quite comic as Yahweh Elohim creates an endless variety of creatures and brings them to The Human. The Human names them all but none are suitable for what is needed. With Yahweh Elohim's special creation of woman, the search comes to a moment of joyful recognition. 'At last!', cries The Human. It is only now, with this gift of companionship, that The Human begins to speak. The Human's own personhood and identity is emerging through relationship. The Human is made for community.

Now, with the creation of woman, the names begin to change. Let me quote these verses in an English version and then with the Hebrew names substituted to illustrate this:

The rib that the Lord God had taken from the man he made into a woman and brought her to the man. Then the man said,

'This at last is bone of my bones
and flesh of my flesh;
this one shall be called Woman,
for out of Man this one was taken.' (Gen. 2.22–23)

The rib that the Yahweh Elohim had taken from The Human
he made into Ish-ah and brought her to The Human. Then
The Human said,
'This at last is bone of my bones
and flesh of my flesh;
this one shall be called Ish-ah,
for out of Ish this one was taken.'

The humans are now male and female, but still personally
unnamed.

The story now tells of the temptation and fall. Woman is
just called *ish-ah* or 'his wife'. The man is The Human or, just
once, her 'husband'. Throughout the conversation between the
woman and the snake, the story reverts to the former name
for God – Elohim. But after the catastrophe that follows their
disobedience it is Yahweh Elohim who comes looking for them.

Judgement is pronounced upon them and The Human and
the woman, now called his wife, have left the garden. Two final
name changes now occur as this creation drama concludes.
Only now, in exile, as the woman becomes pregnant, does The
Human personally name her Eve, 'because she was the mother
of all who live' (v. 20). So it is that in the exile that the story
calls death, Eve is named as life-giver.

And now the name of God changes one final time. Yahweh
Elohim becomes just 'Yahweh'. From this point the stories are
led by the personal, revealing, relating, covenant-making God
whose name is 'I AM'.

Naming and being named is central to our personhood and to
knowing and being known in community. As this story unfolds
the evolution of these names is a way the story subtly traces
how understanding and relationships are growing and developing. Only after Adam becomes aware of Eve as a person and
names her, does a clearer sense of God as personal emerge in

the story too. Adam's own personhood also now emerges and he receives his own personal name at last. The Human becomes Adam, the man.

19

Talking to a Snake

Desire and temptation

Now the serpent was more crafty than any other wild animal that the Lord God had made. He said to the woman, 'Did God say, "You shall not eat from any tree in the garden"?' The woman said to the serpent, 'We may eat of the fruit of the trees in the garden; but God said, "You shall not eat of the fruit of the tree that is in the middle of the garden, nor shall you touch it, or you shall die."' But the serpent said to the woman, 'You will not die; for God knows that when you eat of it your eyes will be opened, and you will be like God, knowing good and evil.' So when the woman saw that the tree was good for food, and that it was a delight to the eyes, and that the tree was to be desired to make one wise, she took of its fruit and ate; and she also gave some to her husband, who was with her, and he ate. Then the eyes of both were opened, and they knew that they were naked; and they sewed fig leaves together and made loincloths for themselves. (Gen. 3.1–7)

One day, naked and not ashamed, Eve and Adam bump into the snake in the garden and they strike up a conversation – the first one recorded in the Bible. Perhaps this had become a pleasurable habit of theirs in the cool of the evening. Either way, the garden is revealed as a world in which there is talking, wondering, thinking, debating, questioning, challenging, remembering and exploring. This is surely good. Growing, maturing and understanding requires this.

The snake is introduced as a creature – more cunning than any of the animals – but still just a creature. No evil persona is attached to it. This is not Satan. Moreover, nothing suggests the conversation itself was wrong at this point. We may imagine the snake was a stimulating and intelligent conversation partner. 'Crafty' can also be translated 'clever', 'cunning' and 'shrewd'.

The stress on the snake as a creature means the responsibility in this story stays with the humans. Some punning is going on, a favourite device in Bible storytelling, but not easy to spot in translation. In the Hebrew, 'cunning' puns on the word 'naked'. As Adam and Eve were not ashamed of their nakedness, we are left to ponder what the punning is suggesting. What is being hinted at? Since the knowledge of good and evil is the central issue in this story, does their unashamed nakedness suggest naivety or innocence? The capability to feel shame is actually a quality, and an important guide in discernment.

This is a story about temptation, which in the religious world tends to be only thought of as bad. It may be. And so it becomes here. But more generally temptation is a daily fact of life: it goes with the necessary tasks of considering and choosing between certain alternatives, ways of thinking, or courses of action, and the testing of desire. The outcomes may be good or bad; very often it is a mixture of the two. Life is not simple. We experience temptation because this world presents us with creative possibilities and difficult dilemmas. A world without temptation would be a world without choices. The task is to make *wise* choices and the storyteller warns us that this requires, above all else, the willingness to obey.

The narrator turns pastoral psychologist and offers a short case study in managing temptation and illicit desire.

The snake begins with a question. 'Did God say you shall not eat from any tree in the garden?' Was that a rumour going round the creatures? The question need not be an invitation to doubt. 'What did he *actually* say?' is often an important starting point. I am hearing-impaired. I know the importance of checking if I have heard accurately. Ellen Davis notes that 'it is fairly rare in biblical narrative for one character to quote another character directly; when it does happen, the quote should be checked for accuracy' (Davis, 2019, p. 30). The woman was not even there when God spoke those words. Did Adam report correctly? (Adam is present for all this, by the way, but is silent throughout.) Is the snake asking for clarification or is this subtle mind games?

The woman clarifies: it was *not* a ban on all fruit trees, but she extends the original prohibition by adding, 'You shall not touch it.' This is significant. In ancient storytelling, words are not changed lightly. It suggests that this tree has already caught her attention as well. Knowing that the beautiful fruit there must not be eaten, she still wants to get a little bit nearer. 'Can I just touch it?' It is often remarked that the surest way to induce someone to want something is to tell them they cannot have it. Suddenly, nothing becomes more attractive or desirable. There is vulnerability, and now the snake pushes back hard, directly challenging the truth of what God has said. 'You will not die; for God knows that when you eat of it your eyes will be opened, and you will be like God, knowing good and evil' (Gen. 3.4–5). He is surely speaking aloud the thoughts the woman is not admitting to herself.

The storyteller normally stays on the outside, recording events and actions. But now we are taken inside the woman's head and heart. The story is full of words of feeling, desire and movement. 'Eat' is repeated six times, 'eyes' and 'seeing' five times. When the woman 'saw that the tree was good', she is copying God's own assessment of what he has made. She is also right that 'the tree was to be desired to make one wise'. Wisdom is its purpose. But the word 'desire' here is strong. It suggests coveting or even 'lusting after'. She is in too deep. She is now in the grip of powerful desire. God's original unambiguous prohibition is forgotten. She takes the fruit and eats it. So does Adam, whose silence throughout is thoroughly collusive in the face of challenges to God's clear instruction.

Their eyes are indeed opened to the knowledge of good and evil – but also to their nakedness, and to knowledge that is now unbearable to them. The story that began with the man and women naked and not ashamed (Gen. 2.29) ends with them crouching behind shrubs to hide their nakedness, blushing furiously as they try to get the hang of making clothes – a skill they have not needed until now.

Something has gone horribly wrong, the consequences of which have yet to be revealed.

20

The Fall in Four Acts

Descending into sin

Historic Christian faith has focused everything on a moment in the drama that we have called 'The Fall' and the 'Original Sin'. This is where, it is believed, a decisive rupture happened in the history of God's relationship with humanity. This story is telling of the moment sin entered the world.

This idea is so deeply established it comes as a surprise to realize that nowhere in the rest of the Old Testament is any belief to be found that sin entered the world at one moment in time, through one individual's action. In fact, if you were to read the rest of the Hebrew scriptures without knowing anything about this brief story, you would not know it even existed. Sin is taken very seriously, but it is found in a mixed journey of ups and downs. There are moments of ghastly, fallen behaviour, evil and repentance. There are times of profound holiness and glorious faithfulness.

Although the story of the Fall in the garden has come to occupy a central place in the Christian faith, most Bible scholars see the entry of sin in the world as a sequence that runs from chapters 1 to 11 of Genesis. Something profound and tragic happens in the garden but it is told as part of a progressive fall, rather than a single event.

Rabbi Jonathan Sacks speaks of it as a drama in four acts (2019, pp. 61ff).

Act 1: Adam and Eve – the failure of personal responsibility

Having taken the fruit forbidden to them, their disobedience is followed by an inability to take responsibility for their actions.

THE FALL IN FOUR ACTS

Their shame could be redemptive but they try to hide instead. Confronted by God, the man blames the woman, she blames the snake. This is the earliest example of victim culture.

Act 2: Cain and Abel – a failure of moral responsibility (Genesis 4)

We are now outside the garden and, despite the judgements and curses that tipped Adam and Eve out of paradise, life seems strangely normal. They bear a child and call him Cain, meaning 'get', or 'acquire'. Eve is acknowledging a gift of God. God seems to be as present for good, as much outside the garden, as within. A second son follows, Abel.

All seems well until both sons offer sacrifices to God but only Abel's is accepted. We are not told why. The focus is on how Cain manages his deep resentment and anger. God is present to advise him. 'Why are you angry, sin is lurking at the door; its desire is for you, but you must master it' (Gen. 4.6). This is the first time the word 'sin' appears in the Bible. It seems that whatever happened in the garden, humanity can still overcome temptation in this world. But Cain kills Abel. When God asks him where Abel is, he lies and denies responsibility. 'I do not know; am I my brother's keeper?' Yes, Cain, you are. We all are.

Act 3: Noah and the ark and a failure of collective responsibility (Genesis 6—9)

A considerable time has passed and the world has become a place of such comprehensive wickedness that God regrets creating it and wonders whether to end it. He responds not as a grieving parent wounded over the lost relationship. His pain is described with the same word that tells of Eve's pain in childbirth. But rather than end or abandon the world, God chooses to begin again with a man called Noah.

Noah is introduced with great hopes and he survives the flood. But Jonathan Sacks insists that, from a Jewish perspective, Noah is a disappointment. 'What does Noah say to God when the decree is issued that the world is about to perish?

What does he say when he was told to make an ark to save himself and his family? What does he say when the rain begins to fall? The answer is nothing. Instead we read, four times, of his silent obedience' (Sacks, 2019, p. 45). Crucially, Noah does not save or redeem anyone except himself, and in the Jewish faith no one is saved individually. Salvation is for all, or none.

Act 4: The Tower of Babel – the failure of ontological responsibility (Genesis 11)

In Genesis 11 we read the strange story of how humanity, now filling the world, planned to build what we would call an enormous skyscraper. It is a story of collective ambition and control – to reach heaven from earth and 'make a name for ourselves' (Gen. 11.4). Like the other acts in this drama there is much more going on. But there are corporate echoes here of the first fall. This is an attempt to be like God. It is a refusal to accept that 'something beyond us makes a call upon us' (Sacks, 2009, p. 63).

This is our human drama too. It begins in childhood, but it is the journey of our lifetime. From our earliest awareness and encounters, we begin to learn what it means to be personally responsible, to make choices, and to act, morally. We must learn, for example, that just because we can, or want to, is not the wisest basis for acting. We begin to explore what it means to take our part in wider society, to know what is ours to do, and seek to fulfil it. Most deeply of all there is the journey of faith. All our living, individually and collectively, finds true meaning in a faithful response to the call of God, who holds us in being.

Our journey into faithfulness, maturity and understanding involves all four acts, not just one. The drama continually leads us to the heart of our human dilemma – our perennial capacity for sinning, falling and failing.

21

Adam and Eve's DNA

Adam, Eve and the evolutionary story

Deep in an extensive cave network in a remote part of East Africa, archaeologists find tiny bone fragments that they believe to be the earthly remains of Adam and Eve. When they extract DNA, what would they find? Cutting edge science meets the Bible.

There is a well-known drawing called 'The Ascent of Man'. It traces a smooth evolutionary arc from a small monkey at the beginning, then progressively larger primates and prehistoric hominins before arriving at the tallest of them all – a recognizably modern man. This is totally misleading. There was no one single evolutionary line, and no one point of human beginning. Our DNA is closest to the chimpanzee but a separation from primates happened over time in deep prehistory. First came the species of (pre)humans called 'hominins'. Fossils of the oldest known hominin, Ardipithecus, were found in Ethiopia, dating back more than five million years. Australopithecus hominins lived between four and two million years ago. Early modern humans were given the prefix 'homo'. Homo habilis, Ergaster, Denisovans and Neanderthal. We now know that, over many thousands of years they coexisted at times and, on occasion, interbred, including with our own ancestor, Homo sapiens. So it is that humans today can trace small percentages of our DNA to Neanderthals, and in parts of East Asia a higher percentage of Denisovan DNA. This means we are descendants of mixed ancestry, including from human species now extinct.

There is still a widespread assumption that Christian faith and science must exist in an awkward and unreconcilable relationship with each other. A certain understanding of the authority and inspiration of the Bible can and does lead to very literal readings of the creation story and therefore a rejection of scientific findings that are thought to contradict this. In the most literal reading Adam and Eve were a unique creation by God, fully formed in every way, and having no biological ancestors. Their historic DNA account would have therefore been empty. They were, therefore, the original parents of the new human species. All humanity today are direct descendants from this couple. The genealogical tables in the Bible all track back to Adam. Do not Jesus and St Paul speak of Adam as a historic person? This was the position of Victorian natural historian and scientist Philip Gosse. He acknowledged his research into fossils suggested clear evidence that the natural world was of great age. Gosse was also a deeply committed Christian with a passionate commitment to the Bible. For him, the revealed word of God must come first. He believed the Bible taught that God made the world complete, in a moment, but with all the appearance of age – such as rock strata, tree rings and even a navel for Adam.

In fact, these more literal readings of the creation story are relatively modern, and in some ways the outcome of a rational, scientific mindset. The early church theologians, for example, were comfortable with more figurative, non-literal readings. Nor are faith, Bible and science in conflict. Today there are flourishing networks where scientists, geneticists, biologists and theologians meet and engage around the issues of understanding and belief. BioLogos is one example. Working from an evangelical foundation with a strong commitment to the Bible, it offers extensive resources exploring the 'harmony between science and biblical faith as we present an evolutionary understanding of God's creation' (BioLogos).

On one key point there is widespread acceptance. Except by the totally miraculous intervention of God, Adam and Eve could not be the first couple of a new species. The genetic diversity of human beings today makes it impossible for us to have descended from just one couple, but rather from many, and over a long period of time.

So what possibilities are there for integrating biblical teaching with the witness of scientific evidence? Theologian and biologist Denis Alexander offers two examples of how this might be done. They take the form of broad models for exploring an understanding of what may have happened. We do not actually know of course. The models come in variant versions and both face challenges and criticisms as part of the continuing debates. Models are ways of exploring not explaining. We are learning as we go (Alexander, 2010).

The 'Retelling Model' is based upon what is called a gradualist view. In Africa, around 200,000 years ago, various species of early humans were evolving and developing – cognitively, culturally, linguistically and in spiritual awareness. This included a natural occurring and growing awareness of God's presence and calling upon their lives. This is called 'general revelation' and finds support in St Paul's writing. 'Ever since the creation of the world his eternal power and divine nature, invisible though they are, have been understood and seen through the things he has made' (Rom. 1.20).

The 'Homo Divinus' model is also situated before history as normally understood. It also looks for actual events that might correspond to the biblical account but works more closely with the detail that the Genesis story provides. Adam and Eve, in this view, were real people, living in a particular historical era and geographical location. Thus, at a certain stage of human evolution and development, there was a moment when God entered into a special relationship with a couple (or community in one variant) and called them to be the parents of a newly emerging humanity in his image. Hence the name Homo Divinus.

These are two models among many, with each playing their part in an ongoing discussion. Both are theologically exploratory and questioning, seeking to faithfully interpret the Bible in the light of scientific knowledge. This reminds us, if we need it, that Christians who are committed to the Bible as their central guide can and do hold differing views on what they believe the Bible teaches, and why.

The discussion has barely begun. Whether through a specific action, a moment in history, or a steady process over time, no less deadly in consequence, something happens in the first creation. Life for the newly created Adam and Eve and their world becomes a place of sin, suffering, death and evil. How are we to understand this? To this we turn over the next few chapters.

22

In the Cool of the Evening

On freedom and obedience

They heard the sound of the Lord God walking in the garden at the time of the evening breeze, and the man and his wife hid themselves from the presence of the Lord God among the trees of the garden. (Gen. 3.8)

It was always the loveliest time to be in the garden. The harsh heat of the day has eased. The light is softening on the trees in the late sun. The air is fresh on the evening breezes. Have you noticed that when God created days he did not even bother with afternoons? There was just evening and morning (Gen. 1.5). No one goes out in the heat of the day if they can avoid it. It was siesta time in that part of the world. Even God does not appear until the cool of the evening.

Here is a tender, if brief, glimpse of the kind of relationship God seeks with his human creation. He has come looking for their company. Wondering what they have been up to? How the day has gone for his new creation? The mood is trusting, but he cannot find them. They had heard him coming and 'hid themselves from the presence of the Lord God among the trees of the garden'. 'Where are you?' he calls. Does he really not know what has just happened? His questions imply that he does not. But doesn't God know everything? Let's leave that one; this is how stories work. Talking of God in this way is called anthropomorphic.

This is a wisdom tale. What is it telling us?

Eden is a garden of generous permissions and immense freedoms. But at the centre is one solitary negative in the form of a particular tree and a firm prohibition. It is there for a good reason; God knows what he is about. To eat from that tree is death. Remember, the boundary is not there to restrict life but to enable its freedom. The garden is not an authoritarian regime. God is not an autocrat. The command is not coercive. He is not possessive of personal property. The concern is entirely pastoral.

Rabbi Jonathan Sacks observes that while there are 613 commands in the Torah (the first five books of the Bible), the Hebrew language had no word for 'obey'. Modern Hebrew had to create a word for outright obedience. The Hebrew words *shema* and *lishmoa* (regularly translated 'obey') are a call to hear, listen, attend, understand. Sacks suggests that God seeks from us 'a greater virtue than obedience'. He seeks our *responsibility* (Sacks, 2019, p. 45).

Being responsible requires trust, and trust is not automatic. We learn it through relationship. From our earliest experiences of life we find it is not risk-free and once trust is broken it is only restored with great difficulty. Two-thirds of the psalms start from precisely such experiences of loss and pain. Even our experience of God can let us down.

This story is interpreted in different ways. In the more literal readings Adam and Eve were created complete: fully developed morally, emotionally and physically. Therefore, when they 'fall' it is clearly their fault. They simply should have known better. When discussing sin and its consequences the language therefore tends to be of trespass, law breaking, debt, guilt and punishment.

The story is approached from a more pastoral perspective in the Eastern Orthodox tradition. The starting place is God's original intention. Andrew Louth writes:

If what God wants is a loving union between himself and the human beings he has made then these beings need to learn to love. They cannot be created knowing what that means: it is something that comes from experience, either innocent experience or (as turned out to be the case) an experience that has to learn by its mistakes. God created human beings that need to learn to love; he created a beginning that needed to move towards fulfilment. (Louth, 2013, p. 69)

God is asking them to listen and to take responsibility.

The distinction is sometimes made between image and likeness. Humanity is created in the image of God but needs to grow, develop and mature into his likeness. This takes time and is learned through hard-won and mixed experience. So could the story have unfolded in any other way? This has led some to treat that first transgression as the stumbling of children, of immaturity, rather than the wilfulness of adults who have no excuse. The language of sin and salvation centres more on meeting, healing, restoring relationship and union with God.

If this story is simply about authority, then the response required is obedience.

If the story is about being responsible, the situation requires trust. That is not automatic; we are not born with it. Trust is something we learn. The warning in this story is that it is impossible for anyone to gain the responsible knowledge of self, the world and the wisdom to live in it, apart from a humble, trusting, yielding to God's guiding word.

Back in the garden, God quickly uncovers what they have done. What he encounters is a total breakdown of trust and a failure to take responsibility for their actions. All that the world was created to be has gone into reverse. Hiding in the bushes to cover their nakedness, they respond only with avoidance, denial and blame.

There is a simple directness to the focus of this story. It is concerned with how to live in God's world on God's terms. Not because God is possessive and controlling. Quite the reverse. We are being offered a way of freedom and fellowship. But this requires our responsible, trusting obedience. There is no alternative world on offer.

23

Eve

Mother of all life

*The man named his wife Eve, because she was the mother of
all who live.* (Gen. 3.20)

Eve deserves at least a chapter of her own. She occupies a unique
place in the creation story. No one else's creation is greeted
with such overwhelming joy and delight. Adam was crafted
out of the earth. The word that describes God making Eve is
used of skilled designers. She is also given the most positive of
all names. Eve means 'mother of all living'. She is joy-giving,
companion-making and life-giving, made in the image of God.

The Human lacked a helper/companion who will become the
means by which the earth creature will grow into full humanity.
The Human is not yet a human being. But Eve is more than
simply a response to a need. She is a second act of creation that
fulfils and completes the first. We explored the meaning of the
word for her role – '*ezer*' (helper) – in Chapter 16. As so often,
the narrator offers only the bare outline. We have to go looking
somewhere else to find illustrations of what this *ezer* might look
like in practice. Possibly the clearest example in the scriptures
of what Adam was seeking is found in the tribute to the wife
in the last chapter of the book of Proverbs. The NRSVA translation succeeds in patronizing her. 'A capable wife who can
find?' (Prov. 31.10). But this is someone far more than com-
petent. The Hebrew word is altogether stronger. It can refer to
valiant military action. Jewish readings and songs call her the
'valorous wife'. Her life and gifts are celebrated in the language
of fulsome praise and grateful mutuality. 'In Hebrew scripture
this is the most unambiguously, flattering portrait of any indi-

vidual, man, or woman' (Davis, 2004, p. 151). She is in every way her husband's equal or more. The list of her achievements in management, business, finance and much else is long and varied but without, surprisingly, any mention of her fertility, childbearing or motherhood. Her children only appear at the end, where they stand with her husband and praise and bless her (Prov. 31.28).

Most strikingly of all, she is portrayed as the personification of Lady Wisdom herself. In Proverbs, God's word and presence is expressed through a wholly positive image of a woman.

All of which is in sharp contrast to the way Eve is more often remembered. In Michelangelo's painting of the temptation scene in the garden, Eve is receiving the fruit from the snake while Adam is simply helping himself. Religious art in those times often painted the serpent with a woman's face. Michelangelo goes further. The serpent is painted as a woman from the waist up. Following the common assumption that the serpent is Satan he depicts Eve as the devil incarnate. This reflects the treatment and depiction of women in the greater part of religious history ever since. Origen called women 'the devil's gateway'. The legacy of that belief has been appalling for women, justifying their exclusion in church and society, their silencing, persecution, and has given rise to prejudicial assumptions about the character of the 'weaker sex'.

When it comes to apportioning blame for what happened, the story shows no interest in gender at all. What happened involved them both. Both were held responsible. The rest of the Old Testament makes virtually no reference to them at all. In the entire Bible only one verse appears to lay the blame on Eve. 'For Adam was formed first, then Eve; and Adam was not deceived, but the woman was deceived and became a transgressor' (1 Tim. 2.13–14). How are we to understand this?

Elsewhere in his writings, Paul clearly affirms the equality of men and women, and names and greets women as prophets, teachers and apostles in the church. He is not contradicting himself. In his letter to Timothy he is addressing particular conflicts between women and men in the church in Ephesus. Ephesus was a city dominated by the huge temple to the goddess

Artemis. This cult was led by women and hostile to men, who could only participate if they were first castrated. Women were used to being dominant in that religion and society. Men were routinely despised and marginalized. Imagine the problems when women converts joined the church from that cult.

Firm pastoral guidance was needed. First, says Paul, 'Let a woman learn' (v.11). This was very new in both the Jewish and gentile society of his day. Education was only for men. Paul is being radically affirming of women. He is also being very practical. He has no objection to women leading and teaching – but they need to have been taught and equipped for the task first. Until that has happened, 'I permit no woman to teach or to have authority over a man' (v.11). To have authority over means 'to lord it over'. To boss. In other churches, Paul is fiercely critical of domineering men misleading the faithful through heretical teaching. Here the problem is with some of the women.

Paul underpins all this with that statement about Eve. 'The woman was deceived and became a transgressor' (vv.13–14). Is Paul saying it was all Eve's fault? There is another possible explanation. This was a culture where some women claimed superiority and men were despised. It is possible that, for lack of clear Christian teaching ('let them learn'), some believed men were to blame for the sin and ills of the world. Imagine, for example, how Paul's statement, 'As in Adam all die' (Rom. 5.15, NIV), might be understood in the church in Ephesus. It is the man's fault. Paul counters any such view by revisiting the story in Genesis with a bold statement, 'Eve was a transgressor!' meaning she *also* is to be blamed, not only Adam.

Eve transgressed. So did Adam. They must live with the loss, shame, pain and exile. But it is in the land of exile, in the shadow that is the consequence of their sin, she receives the most positive name of all: 'The mother of all living'.

24

Adam's Sin and Ours

As in Adam all die

Do we really need the doctrine of Original Sin to convince us there is a serious problem? In his book *Unapologetic*, Francis Spufford called it 'the human propensity to f**k things up' (2013, p. 27). '"Sin" is a label that people now find hard to hear,' he says elsewhere, 'but it is in fact an accurate and straightforward label for very obvious human self-destructive stuff which is part of everyone's life' (Tomkins, 2013).

In the Bible this is understood as a matter far deeper than trying to correct unhelpful habits. Something disabling is at work at every level. St Paul laments that, 'The power of sin within me keeps sabotaging my best intentions. I can will it, but I can't *do* it. I decide to do good, but I don't *really* do it; I decide not to do bad, but then I do it anyway' (Rom. 7.19–20, The Message).

Read literally or more figuratively, we have already noted how the Christian faith reads the story of Adam and Eve's transgression in the garden as the entry point of sin into the whole world. We have also noted that the story itself does not actually say this. Nor, anywhere in the Old Testament as a whole, is Adam's disobedience described as the cause of universal human sinfulness. The Hebrew scriptures express the problem in other ways.

So where did sin begin? For some the question is irrelevant – this is *everyone*'s story. Others imagine, say, a farming couple (or community), perhaps up to 200,000 years ago, to whom God reveals himself and calls them to be the progenitors of a new humanity in his image, revealing his will and purpose for the world. But they turned away. Was it a decisive moment or should we be thinking of a longer process? How did fallenness spread? Like a deadly infection caught by all and from which there is no immunity? Augustine, surely betraying one of his personal anxieties, believed sin was passed on through sexual intercourse, even within a faithful marriage that desired children. He believed newborn babies entered life sharing Adam's guilt and sin, and were destined for hell unless they were baptized. Augustine gave the doctrine of Original Sin its definitive expression in the Western Church. He taught that Adam was the Federal Head of humanity. When Adam fell, all humanity fell with him. What happens to one, happened to all.

Ask those sitting around a table what sin is and you will tend to get a list of wrong thoughts, feelings and actions. At first glance that describes the sin in the Garden. They were tempted, disobeyed and took the fruit. Sin is thus trespass, law-breaking and theft. Theological responses to this tend to borrow metaphors from criminal law courts. The sinner is in the dock. The verdict is guilty. The sentence is death.

Approached like that, sin is actually trivialized. The diagnosis has not gone deep enough. Who we think we are comes before what we do. Our choices, desires and actions flow from our sense of personal identity. Real sin, the sin that is still 'original', is at root the attempt to be what we are not, a desire for a life other than the one we are given. It is ultimately the pursuit of something that does not exist. Life unfolds thereafter as the misguided wanderings of a tragically mistaken identity.

Sin must actually be a desire for the good. What else was on offer in the Garden to desire? The knowledge of good and evil is a right and responsible wisdom to seek. But it was approached as a bid to be who they were not: to be like God, trying to seize what could only be given. For Thomas Merton, sin is an issue of a true and false self:

> To say I was born in sin is to say I came into this world with a false self. I came into existence under a sign of contradiction, being someone that I was never intended to be and therefore a denial of what I am supposed to be. And thus, I came into existence and non-existence at the same time because from

the very start I was something that I was not. (Merton, 1972, p. 33)

Underpinning the understanding of sin in the Bible is a belief in the solidarity of it all – we are made one with each other, with our world and with God. It is a concept that contemporary society struggles to make sense of, with its highly individualistic philosophies. Christian faith has also tended to focus on the sins of the individual. We often have difficulty with the idea of shared consequence and responsibility, especially for the failed actions of others. To be required to share in the negative outcomes of someone else's behaviour is 'not fair'. We apportion blame instead. The idea that we belong to each other, for good or ill, is foreign. All of which is a feature of fallen life in the garden – blame, separation, avoidance, hiding and denial of shared responsibility.

This is what the story calls 'Death' – a radical, utterly traumatic separation from the life originally given and intended with God in creation.

How interesting that so many of the stories we heard in our earliest years circle around themes of lost life and false identity. All those folk stories and fables of people who through their own folly or the mischief or evil of others are helplessly imprisoned in a life of falsity and death. All those ugly ducklings that were really beautiful swans, those frogs who were really handsome princes. The scullery maid who was really the king's true love. Life trapped in non-life. What is needed is the kiss of one whose love is true. That changes everything.

We know all this is true. The stories tell us it is so.

25

Because You Have Done This ...

Judgement and exile

The Lord God said ...
  'Because you have listened to the voice of your wife,
    and have eaten of the tree
  about which I commanded you,
    "You shall not eat of it",
  cursed is the ground because of you;
    in toil you shall eat of it all the days of your life.'
The Lord God sent him forth from the garden of Eden, to till
the ground from which he was taken. He drove out the man;
and at the east of the garden of Eden he placed the cherubim,
and a sword flaming and turning to guard the way to the tree
of life. (Gen. 3.14, 17, 24)

The story is now moving to its conclusion. God has flushed out
Adam and Eve from the bushes where they were hiding. They
must hear the consequences of their actions.

Everything has gone into reverse. Their transgression has
changed everything.

Blessings are replaced by curses. 'Cursed are you' (Gen. 3.14
and 17). Fruitful soil now becomes stony and unyielding. 'Thorns
and thistles it shall bring forth for you' (Gen. 3.18). Harmony
between humans and the creatures under their care becomes
discord: 'I will put enmity between you and the woman' (3.15).
Human mutuality has become patriarchal and hierarchical. 'He
shall rule over you', the woman is told (3.16).

For both, the work intended to be fulfilling has become weary-
ingly hard. 'In toil you shall eat of it all the days of your life',
the human is told (3.17). 'In pain you shall bring forth children'

(3.16), the woman is told. 'Toil' and 'pain' are the same word in the Hebrew. Together they share in a life of painful labour.

Despite this, creation after what is called the Fall seems to be a place of growing and developing. Here, at last, the human and the woman receive their own identity in the form of personal names. The woman's name is remarkably honouring. After being complicit in an action whose consequence was declared to be 'death', she is named Eve – 'mother of all life'. The narrator finally gives 'Adam' his personal name (Gen. 4.26). Only now, apparently, do they consummate their relationship. There is no mention of sexual relations until after sin enters the world.

God is constantly around, though. His care is more specific and practical than at any point in the story so far. He acts to alleviate needs that are the direct consequence of the rebellion. The humans had made makeshift coverings for their nakedness, but God makes clothes for them out of animal skins. In the place we were told would be death, no one has actually died, and God is in a caring relationship with them and guiding them. What is called 'The Fall' plainly does not mean we are unable to do any good or that God is absent. It is not a place of helpless depravity. Although sin has entered the world, the story of Cain, for example, makes clear that humans can still choose to obey and resist sin – and God is to be found encouraging him to do just that (Gen. 4.6–7). Obedience to God is possible.

We might notice that life after the Fall looks very much like the world of a farming couple in poorer parts of the rural Middle East even today. That is exactly what is intended. The soil is poor. Growing enough food and making a living is endlessly hard work. The lack of basic health care and effective contraception means pregnancy and childbirth is painful and life-threatening. But children are their future security and sexual pleasure part of the gift in their life together. 'Your desire will be for your husband' (3.16). The extended use of 'the woman' and 'the human' suggest they are representing all human life. Only at this point do they become named people in their own right.

The garden story could function as a reverse dream. The farmer leans wearily on his plough under the scorching sun.

His wife is recovering from the latest difficult birth and needing strength to run the home and much else. If there were time and energy to ponder, one question might well be – is this how life is meant to be?

Calling this story a 'Fall' can be misleading, but it is hard to find a better name.

There was no fall from a previous life, though. Talking up what life was like in some original state of blissful perfection has been a way of trying to convince people of the terrible effects of sin and their need for salvation. No such place of perfection actually existed. That is not the story being told. It would be more true to say this is a world that has not reached its destiny. If there is a fall, it is falling short, rather than a falling from. 'All have sinned and fall short of the glory of God' (Rom. 3.23).

Now comes an incident that if it were not so serious would be quite amusing. Only now, apparently, does it dawn on God that the couple are still in the garden with full access to everything. Something needs to be done, and quickly. 'What if he [Adam] now should reach out and take fruit from the Tree of Life and eat, and live forever? Never – this cannot happen!' (3.22–24, The Message). Like the original prohibition, God's response is not out of jealousy or possessiveness. God is making a vital pastoral provision for the humans' own good and protection.

To eat from the tree of life and become immortal, knowing good and evil while in a state of falsity and lost identity, would be a kind of living death for them. The doors are promptly shut fast. Heavenly beings with flaming swords guard the entrance. Olivier Clement suggests the significance of this: 'Death is both the result of their transgression but also its remedy, since it makes humanity aware of its finiteness and lays it open to grace' (Clement, 1995, p. 85). God is being kind.

Life beyond the garden – our world – is revealed as a place of mercy.

26

What's Love Got to Do With It?

Evolution and creation

When I look at your heavens, what are mortals that you care for them? (Ps. 8.1–3)

Chet Reymo, the American physicist, astronomer and naturalist, tells of when he witnessed an accident from a distance, while walking in the park. A skateboarder crashed full speed into a young girl. The impact flung her into the air before she landed in a crumpled heap and lay motionless. Reymo continues his relating of the incident from the perspective of the universe:

> During the time she was in the air, the spinning earth carried her half a mile to the east. The motion of the Earth about the Sun, carried her back again, 40 miles westward. The drift of the solar system among the stars of the Milky Way bore her silently 20 miles towards the star, Vega. The turning pinwheel of the Milky Way galaxy carried her 300 miles in a great circle about the galactic centre. (Reymo, 1985)

He saw it all from a distance, so it all happened in complete silence. That was what disturbed him: the silence of the universe at that moment. 'There was no protest from the sky' (Reymo, 1985, pp. 3, 15).

There, in microcosm, one afternoon on Boston Common, our human dilemma is laid out on the hard ground. Innocent suffering and the pitiless indifference of the cosmos collides.

Dante's God is 'the love that moves the sun and the other stars'. The psalmist was likewise inspired when looking up into the night sky:

When I look at your heavens, the work of your fingers,
  the moon and the stars that you have established;
what are human beings that you are mindful of them,
  mortals that you care for them?
Yet you have made them a little lower than God,
  and crowned them with glory and honour.
You have given them dominion over the works of your hands;
  you have put all things under their feet. (Ps. 8.1–3)

Even Job was lifted from his anguished depths of suffering, and reduced to wonder and penitential silence, by his tour of creation with God.

We know so much more than any of them about earth and space today. Awe and wonder are exhausted before the sheer scale of it all, and it keeps increasing by the minute. Earth is just one of up to 400 billion stars and planets in our Milky Way galaxy, which is simply one of an estimated 200 billion to two trillion galaxies in observable space. The light from one galactic nucleus alone has taken a staggering 12 billion years to reach detectors on earth. Telescopic images give us achingly beautiful glimpses from the farthest reaches of space, the birthing and dying of stars, of unimaginably turbulent forces, black holes and dark matter. Add to that our awareness of the vast scale of seeming waste, suffering and death on earth and it may become much harder, not easier, to imagine all this as the work of something we call love. Reymo is right when he says it takes courage to open ourselves to all this, but that is what we have to do if we are to know who we truly are (Reymo, 1985, p. ix). We must risk the spiritual vertigo, as 'we are joy-riding on a speck of dust' in the slip-stream of this wildly expanding universe (Taylor, 1992, p. 179).

So where does the idea of love come from in a world formed from random collisions of gases and matter and game-changing coincidences in the timeless voids of deep space? The word 'love' does not appear in the creation stories but the Bible is full of it. 'God is love' is the nearest we have to a biblical definition of the divine (1 John 4.7).

If the language of love belongs here at all it must undergo a profound conversion of understanding. When humans are created in the image of the God who is love something new is transcending functional evolutionary processes. Love is not concerned with survival, nor about ensuring who is the fittest. Love calls us to a quite new way of knowing ourselves, one another and our world. 'There need be no surprises if this phase of creation, not now in the making of inanimate rock, ocean, but of men and women striving towards their completion, is also, and even more, turbulent and restless' (Elphinstone, 1976, p. 30). The path of love is both harder and more glorious than the paths to survival pursued by evolution. If it is God's love, then it must be the way of the cross and pain, suffering and death. All play their part.

The seemingly unnecessary, cruel, offensive wastefulness of evolutionary processes proves to be quite the reverse. We now know the universe has to be the size it is to sustain this life of ours at all. If it were only the size of our solar system it would barely last an hour. Far from being a waste, it is revealed as a generous gift. Its very finitude is the source of life's continual renewing through death and new birth. We owe our lives to the fact that this is a world that dies. Life is enabled through death. Every particle of our being and our surrounding world is the gift of the dusty, explosive fallout of dying stars at unimaginable distances. In this world death is necessary for life. Anywhere else this would be heard as the language of sacrificial love. The idea of a deathless, pain-free, perfect paradise from which this all fell is a wishful fantasy. At this point love may be calling us to grow up. Though some, I recognize, have had no choice in the matter.

Creation is not safe and secure because it is part of a controlled programme of progress and development. It is not. Creation is sustained and ever renewed, through life and death, because it is held in a love that 'bears all things, believes all things, hopes all things, endures all things' (1 Cor. 13.7).

27

The Wound of Becoming

What this demands of us

There was a time when life was a struggle for me. I won't bore you with the details. Someone gave me a book. Although I had little energy for reading I opened it at the first page. The first sentence said, 'Life is difficult.' That was all I needed to hear! It was liberating because it gave permission for the way my life was. No other reason was needed. I was burdened with guilt and self-blame for not being what a Christian adult *should* be – trusting, hopeful, joyful, near to God, etc. In fact, God was a significant part of the problem at the time.

The Bible contains a simple guide to life. Do good and you will be blessed. Do wrong and it will go wrong. 'If you obey the Lord your God blessings will come on you ... if you do not obey the Lord your God ... curses will come on you' (from Deut. 28). As a very general principle for living in God's ways it makes sense. But this teaching was behind the disciple's question when they noticed a blind man. 'Who sinned, this man or his parents, that he was born blind?' (John 9.2–3). There must be a reason. If God has cursed a person, someone, somewhere, must have sinned.

As we know, parts of the Bible engage – and even argue – with other parts. This is one example. After all, it is plainly not the case that everything always goes well for good people, and it is also the case that many evil people prosper and live long. The best-known illustration of this argument is Job. His story functions as a theological critique of this over-simple blessing or cursing equation. To set it up, Job is introduced as a man of unimpeachable goodness, devotion and faithfulness. This means that nothing in what follows has anything to do with deserving or guilt. His friends, though, have no other lens through which to view what is happening. He is suffering appallingly, so he *must* have done something wrong. God has plainly stopped blessing. But God does not make this assumption when he finally appears and speaks to Job, and Jesus refused to link blindness to sin at all. Job is a theological reflection on human suffering, pain and death without the language or assumptions of 'The Fall'. This is undeserved suffering. Although sin is a central and serious reality in this world, the Bible does not drop every experience of ill into that basket. Nor should we.

It is hard to imagine a life that involves growing up, maturing and developing responsibility that does not include the experience of risk, pain, struggle, bewilderment, mistakes and loss. Despite the best of intentions, things go wrong. Transitions through the most natural and 'good' stages of life are all marked by degrees of turbulence and uncertainty, and may be as frightening as they are exciting. It may be that we only receive this gift of life as a wound. We each have our own stories of this.

In Chapter 10 I described one of several sculptures of God and Adam on the walls of Chartres Cathedral. They were enjoying the sabbath together. In one of the other sculptures Adam is half emerged from the ground, slumped against God's knee. He looks completely exhausted. I have a photograph of this sculpture on my study wall and sometimes I look and wonder, will Adam make it, or is the effort of coming into life just too much? Some know that question all too well. In that sculpture, God's hands are poised very attentively around Adam's head, close but not touching. I often use this picture in retreats and workshops and quite often someone with midwifery experience will observe how, professionally, those hands were positioned exactly where they were needed as the head emerged and the baby prepared for the final push into new life. They are convinced the sculptor was making that connection. So here is God, midwife to the intense, exhausting vulnerability of our journey into becoming who we truly are.

Trusting in God's presence and will is not a belief in a certain outcome. God does not take away the necessary uncertainty that goes with being alive. He leaves us free. Freedom is his most precious, and our most vulnerable, gift. But his love is ever present, like those poised hands, attentive and responsive through all possible outcomes. He promises never to abandon us. Nothing and nowhere is outside his reach. 'I am convinced that neither death nor life, nor anything else in all creation, will be able to separate us from the love of God that is in Christ Jesus our Lord' (Rom. 8.38–39).

Life can be very tough, even when through no obvious fault of our own. The process of becoming wounds us. For one psalmist even the business of trying to do faith had become too much. His prayer ends with this haunting plea to God: 'Turn your gaze away from me, that I may smile again, before I depart and am no more' (Ps. 39.13). God, I need respite care from believing in you! St Paul faced times when 'we were so utterly, unbearably crushed that we despaired of life itself' (2 Cor. 1.8). The majority of the prayers and songs we call the psalms contain significant protest, bewilderment and angry questioning at the way life is and how God seems to be behaving. 'Why?' 'Where are you?' 'Help me.' This is called lament. Lament is not what happens when faith fails. It is a particular response of faith and prayer to God when life is difficult.

A collection of prayers by Jim Cotter includes an imagined response by God to those suffering most deeply under the demands that living in this world can impose. 'Forgive me for having created a world in which so much pain has to be allowed to happen if I am truly to be a God of love and enable you to love with love that is worthy of the name' (Cotter, 1985, p. 86).

28

The Cost of Creating

What this demands of God

In the last chapter we left Adam half emerged from the ground, slumped against God's lap, exhausted with the effort of coming into being. In that sculpture God is sitting still – a large, calm and imposing figure. The scene is caring, but God is not obviously extended by the task either. Is that how creating is for God? Our storyteller tends only to report on the outside of things. Adam's outburst of joy on meeting Eve, and Eve contemplating the fruit, are brief exceptions. Of God's feelings we are told nothing at this point. The sculptor has his own take on it, though, and leaves us a clue. Tucked behind the head of God, where Christian artists usually put a halo, is a circle containing a cross.

What is the cross doing here in that garden of original goodness? The familiar interpretation would be that this is telling us God already knows the world will need saving through the cross of Christ, which is true. That saving work will come at profound cost to God. But when the cross is placed at the beginning of things, as God is bringing his creation to birth, might that not suggest creating comes at a cost to God?

'God is Christlike, in him there is no unChristlikeness at all,' wrote Michael Ramsey (2012, p. 98). 'He is the image of the invisible God' (Col. 1.15), wrote Paul. 'Whoever has seen me has seen the Father,' said Jesus (John 14.9). The saviour reveals the creator. The way God saves reveals the way he creates in the first place. Does Christ's life and ministry suggest a God for whom this work is serene, effortless and painless? Back in the Genesis story, several chapters in, and many generations on, in the world that has degenerated so deeply into sin and evil, we are abruptly told that, 'The Lord was sorry that he had made humankind on the earth, and it grieved him to his heart' (Gen. 6.6). God even contemplates wiping it all out and starting again, but relents. The word 'grieve' can describe strong physical and acute emotional distress. It is the same word God uses when telling Adam and Eve what life would be like after their transgression – the harsh pangs of their labour.

That God loves, delights in, can be hurt by, and weeps over this world is a commonly held belief today. God is love, and love that does not know, share in and endure pain is surely not love at all. So it comes as a surprise to discover that for the greater part of church history, the belief that God experienced such feelings and passions was believed to be heresy. The Doctrine of Impassibility taught that God is above human emotions and vulnerabilities and cannot be changed by them. Impassibility is an easy doctrine to misunderstand. It never meant that God is without feelings. Rather, the doctrine affirms that God is not subject to the *unreliable* emotional passions and unpredictable mood swings so familiar in human living. He does not explode under pressure, for example, and act in violent, irrational ways. God's emotions are true.

History is written by the winners, the saying goes. The same can be true of those who write theology. For centuries, European churches grew and flourished under the patronage of the dominant political and military world powers, in a partnership we call Christendom. The way God was talked about reflected that. Theology tended to emphasize God's supreme and absolute attributes – omnipotence, sovereign authority, invulnerability and perfect will. It was this all-conquering God, upholding the good and vanquishing evil, who was blessing the troops, on both sides, as they marched to their deaths in the carnage of World War One. The sustained, horrific scale of suffering and death through the century that followed made such a focus on power, conquest and victory altogether too insensitive and actually unsayable as a way of speaking of God. Imagining divine power in the likeness of the ambitions of worldly empires has not served us well. The theological focus has shifted towards the contemplation of a God who takes flesh, suffers, shares pain, gives his very life for us and for our salvation.

What other ways might there be of contemplating the nature and ways of a God who creates us in his image?

An artist tells of the costliness of creating a picture – the intense focus required, the total and exhausting self-giving, poured out on to the canvas. The sheer sustained energy the imagination needs. Is their work in the likeness of God?

A sculptor speaks of feeling humbled as they experience the most basic and unpromising of materials becoming something wonderfully new in their hands. Is that an imaging of God?

A woman tells of the fragile wonder and deep vulnerability of growing a child in her womb from conception to birth. There the whole evolutionary process is played out in microcosm. Is bringing to birth an imaging of God?

Or the story told of a surgeon involved in a pioneering eye operation. The task was untried, intricate, immensely complex and with no margin for error. The outcome was a triumph. But after seven hours of intense, uninterrupted concentration, the surgeon was so utterly spent they had to be led from the operating theatre by the hand to rest in a side room. Is that an image of the costly creating work of God? 'Always, for the richness of the creation, God is made poor, and for its fulness, God is made empty' (Vanstone, 1977, p. 97).

In the novel *Peter Abelard* by Helen Waddell, Peter Abelard's friend Thibault is anguishing over the pain of the world. They are walking in the woods and come to a tree that has been felled. Pointing to the sawn end of the trunk, Abelard observes what is revealed there is true along the unseen length of the whole tree. Christ's cross is like that, he says. It reveals what is always true, but unseen, of the eternal life and character of God. The cross, he says, is 'the bit of God that we saw' (Waddell, 1950, p. 269).

29

The Winter is Over

The garden in the Song of Songs

My beloved speaks and says to me:
'Arise, my love, my fair one,
*   and come away; for now the winter is past,*
*   the rain is over and gone.*
The flowers appear on the earth;
*   the time of singing has come,*
and the voice of the turtle-dove
*   is heard in our land.*
The fig tree puts forth its figs,
*   and the vines are in blossom;*
*   they give forth fragrance.'* (Song of Songs 2.10–13)

In the middle of the Bible is a short, erotic love poem called the Song of Songs. Its presence amid the most holy writings of that conservatively religious world continues to surprise. It is startlingly explicit at times. Marriage is not mentioned at all. God makes no appearances. Nor are there any clear references to faith, prayer, worship or religious practice, still less ethics.

This has led some to suggest it is the *least* biblical book in the Bible.

In fact, the Song of Songs is saturated with poetic and symbolic references to the Torah and the Temple – and thus to the very centre of Jewish faith. This is easily missed because the poetic imagery is (literally) foreign to modern ears. The language of the poem is one of ceaseless worship, adoration, petition and longing. This led one of the greatest Jewish rabbis from the first century, Rabbi Akiva, to call this song 'the holiest of holies' – for in this celebration of love and union the whole story of the Bible is being told.

So perhaps it is not surprising to discover that down through history more commentaries have been written about this love poem than any other books in the Bible except Genesis and Psalms. The Jewish people read it as a passionate expression of their love and devotion for the Torah. The Song of Songs is read aloud in its entirety at Passover. The medieval church read it as a contemplation of the love between Christ and his bride, the church. When it is read today the Song is more often caught up in debates about sex and sexuality. But like all good poetry the Song plays at different levels. The imagery weaves together varied meanings and themes.

Of central significance is that the Song is set in a garden. It is no accident that this love story is being played out precisely where the Bible begins and where it went so terribly wrong – the garden from which Adam and Eve were exiled altogether. Something has changed, though. This garden could not be more full of life, fruitfulness and beauty. It is pungent with blossom and vibrant with hopeful, passionate longing.

In the Genesis garden, the breakdown of life from the original goodness was marked by three points of alienation.

There was the alienation between the man and woman. A relationship of delight, mutuality and partnership collapses into the experience of shame, hiding and a patriarchal imbalance of power. 'He shall rule over you' (Gen. 3.16), the woman is told.

There was alienation between humanity and nature. This is marked by hostility between Eve and the snake – 'I will put enmity between you.' It is also expressed by the cursing of the soil that Adam must now toil over to get food. 'Cursed is the ground because of you,' says God (3.18).

The third alienation is at the heart of it all – between humanity and God. 'I was afraid,' says Adam to God, 'and I hid myself' (3.10). All the books of the Bible bear witness in different ways to humanity in exile from God, and to the scars and rents in the fabric of life that are the result of disobedience to God.

In the garden of the Song this is all reversed. The couple embrace in unashamed delight and joyful mutuality. The drama is led throughout by the woman. The richly poetic imagery expresses worship, adoration and divine union. The garden itself is full of life and fragrance and is alive with birdsong. The overwhelming vibrancy and fruitfulness of creation is the constant theme through the poem. When human desire and love finds full expression, in each other and in God, creation itself returns to being the garden of God's gift, presence and delight.

The long exile of humanity is over.

The garden is a vision of what life is meant to be, lived in the fullness of God's presence and original gift – and the hope it may yet be so.

The Song celebrates the reversal of all that was lost in the original garden.

The original threefold rupture is healed – humanity with one another, humanity and God, humanity and nature. The Song's

> ... unique contribution to the biblical canon is to point to the healing of the deepest wounds in the created order, and even the wounds in God's own heart, made by human sin. The Song is about repairing the damage done by the first disobedience in Eden, which the Christian tradition calls 'the Fall'. (Davis, 2004, p. 231)

This poem of passionate desire and intense longing sits between a world long lost and closed to those it was made for, and the world re-created in the love of God. And so do we.

Love, like life itself, is elusive. Though we are most truly made for this, it will take us to our limits and beyond, such that at times we are not sure if it is our ally or adversary. So, while the poem is anticipatory and wonderfully hopeful, it tells of a journey of vulnerable, anguished losing and finding, hoping and longing that love requires.

> I sought him, whom my soul loves,
> but found him not ...
> If you find my beloved tell him this,
> I am faint with love. (Song of Songs 3.1, 5.6–8)

30

The World is a Wedding

Creation in John 1

In the beginning was the Word, and the Word was with God, and the Word was God. He was in the beginning with God. All things came into being through him, and without him not one thing came into being. What has come into being in him was life, and the life was the light of all people. The light shines in the darkness, and the darkness did not overcome it. (John 1.1–5)

John's Gospel begins with a creation story. He starts with the same iconic first words as Genesis. 'In the beginning ...' (1.1). The same themes of light, dark and time are found here. Light has come into the world, in a new and glorious way (1.4–9). The story unfolds day by day.

The divine source of creation, the creating Word through whom everything came into existence, is now revealed. It is Jesus. That he is the source of it all could not be more strongly stressed. Words and phrases like 'beginning', 'came into being', 'coming into being' and 'became' are repeated ten times in relation to him.

This is not a reboot of what happened in the beginning. John is looking forward. Something astonishingly new has begun that he has personally witnessed. The Creator has entered this world as creature. 'The Word became flesh and lived among us, and we have seen his glory' (1.14). This is a new creation, from within.

The world Jesus comes into is characterized as one that does not know him. Apart from John the Baptist, chosen to be 'a witness to testify to the light, so that all might believe through him' (1.6), no one else there has any idea what is going on. There is a repeated emphasis on the inability to understand or recognize what is going on. 'He was in the world, and the world came into being through him; yet the world did not know him' (1.10). John the Baptist is constantly and impatiently pushing back misguided questions and beliefs. 'I am *not* the messiah', 'I am *not*', 'No!', 'You do not know', and other negations come ten times. A world that lost its way in the beginning through a disastrous grab for knowledge is now found to be without the most basic discernment and awareness. 'One stands among you whom you do not know' (1.26). Not only is the Creator a stranger to those he made, his world rejects him. 'He came to what was his own, and his own people did not accept him' (1.11).

Though it takes a bit of detective work, this opening section of John's Gospel is seven days long – like the first creation story. But it comes to its climax at a village wedding on what John calls 'the third day'. The two numbers are highly symbolic. The seventh day is an allusion to the day the original creation was celebrated as being whole and complete with God. The third day points forwards to the day of resurrection and the beginning of the new creation.

Meanwhile, at the wedding, disaster has struck. The wine has run out. How and why, we are not told. All we know is that this unnamed couple and their families face shame and humiliation. Human celebration has run out, at the very beginning, and is unable to renew itself.

If the initial stress in this story was on unknowing, the focus is now on human emptiness and powerlessness. We are entering the heart of this story. Over by the wall were six stone water jars used for religious purification. They are empty. They represent part of the old ordering – the one that had now run out and was empty of power to transform earthly living and awaken celebration. Jesus now acts. 'Fill them up with water,' he commands (2.7).

Here is another overlapping theme. Water was what covered the earth at the beginning. All life comes out of water. Water is, in fact, one of John's favourite themes. His Gospel is full of rivers, wells, jars, vessels, springs, lakes and, finally, the water that poured from Jesus' side on the cross (19.33).

Jesus tells a servant to take a glass of the water, that is now wine, to the chief steward. He tastes it and cannot believe the quality of what he is drinking. 'Everyone serves the good wine first, and then the inferior wine after the guests have become drunk,' he tells the undoubtedly baffled groom. 'But you have kept the good wine until now.' The old has been transfigured by the new. The emptiness of the old filled up by the new. The water of the old is transformed into the wine of the new and becomes a taste of the coming kingdom.

Now creating a large quantity of top-quality wine when everyone there had already drunk freely is not just generous, it is irresponsible! Not only does this new order transform the old, it goes completely over the top.

Finally, John sums up the wedding story and the whole opening sequence of his Gospel. 'Jesus did this, the first of his signs, in Cana of Galilee, and revealed his glory; and his disciples believed in him' (2.11). The translation conceals an important connection. The words translated as 'did' and 'first' are also found in Greek translations of the first verse of Genesis chapter 1. Translated in this way, that verse declares, 'Jesus *created* this, the *beginning* of his signs ...'

And what is this all a sign of? It may be beginning to dawn on John's hearers that this is a story about *two* weddings. Through the blessing of this village wedding with a wildly generous gift of God, a new celebration is being revealed. The steward was right to go to the bridegroom with the new wine, but he went to the wrong one. It was *Jesus* who did this. In a few verses' time John the Baptist will be describing Jesus as the Bridegroom and himself as the best man, proclaiming to all that the wedding celebrations are ready to begin (3.29).

The world is a wedding.

This is the marriage of heaven and earth.

31

Resurrection and Recreation

Easter and beyond

Mary stood weeping outside the tomb ... she turned round and saw Jesus standing there, but she did not know that it was Jesus. Jesus said to her, 'Woman, why are you weeping? For whom are you looking?' Supposing him to be the gardener, she said to him, 'Sir, if you have carried him away, tell me where you have laid him, and I will take him away.' Jesus said to her, 'Mary!' She turned and said to him in Hebrew, 'Rabbouni!' (which means Teacher). (John 20.11–16)

When he was at the table with them, he took bread, blessed and broke it, and gave it to them. Then their eyes were opened, and they recognized him. (Luke 24.30–31)

On either side of Good Friday and the crucifixion of Jesus, the drama centres on two gardens.

The first is the garden of Gethsemane, on the Mount of Olives, just across the valley from Jerusalem. The garden was a favourite place for Jesus and his disciples when they needed some space and rest. It was there, on the night of his betrayal, that Jesus agonized alone over what lay before him (Matt. 26.36–56). In some ways that scene in Gethsemane is like a photographic negative of the original garden of Eden. It is night, not day. A garden of delight and rest is now a place of sleepless anguish and dread. A place of refuge is now a place of deadly danger. Here is grief not joy, betrayal not hospitality, the shadow of death instead of the light of life. It was here that Jesus was arrested and began his final journey to the cross.

The second garden was the private property of a wealthy fol-

RESURRECTION AND RECREATION

lower of Jesus. It contained his own tomb – sometimes a feature of pleasure gardens. He made a gift of it to provide the body of Jesus with a resting place. In that garden Jesus lay in death, and in that garden, on Easter Day, he appears, risen to new life. By the time the body of Jesus was released by the authorities there was not time to complete the prescribed rituals for anointing the dead before the sabbath day began. The world must rest. Even Jesus rests. The ancient service of night prayer recalls this when it speaks of him as the one 'who at this evening hour rested in the tomb and so hallowed the grave to be a bed of hope for all who put their trust in you'.

We can imagine the desperate eagerness of Mary to come back to the tomb. Having honoured the sabbath day, she is there at first light only to find the tomb open, and the body of Jesus gone. She calls the disciples. They come running, confirm the scene, and return home. Mary is left alone outside the tomb, distraught. There is something very authentic and honest about this scene. They would all have been grief-stricken and emotionally exhausted after the events of the previous days. Today we might be speaking of post-traumatic stress.

There is a brief encounter with angels, but Mary is alone again, weeping. A voice behind her asks, 'Why are you weeping?' Mary turns away from the tomb. Away from death. Someone is standing there who she knows so well but now does not recognize. It is Jesus, but she thinks he is the gardener. Perhaps he may know where the body has gone? This will be a familiar theme in the stories that follow. The risen Jesus is not for recognizing by human choice or will. It is for him to reveal himself. A new story is beginning. It requires new eyes.

There is a delightful irony in Mary's confusion over the identity of the stranger. In a quite different sense, she was right to think Jesus was the gardener. Notice how carefully John has set the scene. They are standing in a garden. It is the morning of the first day. This is the beginning of a new creation. Jesus is the new Adam. And he begins, as the first Adam did, by naming creation – 'Mary'. Now Mary turns again but this time in astonished and joyful recognition.

Though a garden is not directly mentioned again, there is

103

one further resurrection story that makes a connection with the original garden in Genesis. It is later on that same Easter Day, and two disciples are to be found walking away from Jerusalem. They are depressed and dispirited. They had heard rumours that Jesus had risen from the dead but could not believe it. They are simply going home. The one they thought was going to change everything was dead. The story is over.

Jesus joins them on the road but, as in the story of Mary, they are not able to recognize him. They talk as they walk and by the time they reach home it is getting dark. They urge the stranger to stay with them.

Later, at the evening meal, Jesus takes the role of host. He takes bread, blesses and breaks it, and gives it to them. 'Then their eyes were opened, and they recognized him' (Luke 24.31).

Only a few days before, Jesus had done just the same thing at the Last Supper. They were surely remembering that? But Luke is pointing to a further connection. The account of the Last Supper does not tell of eyes being opened in recognition. There is only one place in the whole Bible when eyes are opened following the eating of food. It was in the garden of Eden when Eve and Adam took the fruit from the tree forbidden to them. The result was their 'eyes were opened' (Gen. 2) but to shame and loss, not joy.

Here on the far side of death, on the first day of the new age, eyes are opened once again – but this time to glorious recognition and the gift of new life.

That meal symbolizes that the long exile of the human race is over.

32

O Happy Fault!

Sin, the cross and the new creation

At the climax of the Christian gospel there is a strange pause when nothing happens, at least on the surface of things. Between Good Friday and Easter night, Christ's body lies in the tomb. It is the sabbath. Even God keeps it, as he did in the beginning.

The ancient homilies for the Easter night vigils could not resist imagining what Christ was really up to, though. He has descended to the dead – the destiny of fallen humanity. This cannot be on account of his own sin. He had none. He has *freely* descended there, and so can make his life a gift for all. This completely bankrupts the debt-based economy of hell. Meanwhile, Christ is searching for Adam and Eve, as for his lost sheep. There they are, our first parents, in the deepest shadows of eternal death, sitting in lonely exile from all they were ever made for. They look up and there is Christ, the Lord of Glory, holding out the cross to them, by which he has conquered sin and death. 'I did not create you to be held a prisoner in hell,' he tells them, 'Rise from the dead' (*Triduum Sourcebook*, 1983).

Icons of the resurrection pick up the drama from this moment. Christ is rising straight out of the ground like a rocket. Great slabs of stone are simply smashed out of the way and scattered in all directions. Strewn on the ground are open padlocks, bent keys and broken chains. Hell is harrowed and wasted. As Christ emerges in his risen life he is holding an elderly couple firmly by their wrists. They rise with him. It is Adam and Eve. They are looking slightly bewildered. Well, wouldn't you be?

In the most familiar telling of it, a world created as good in the beginning falls into sin and judgement. Jesus comes in our humanity, the second Adam, and by his cross and resurrection wins our forgiveness and deliverance. God thereby offers us an incredibly costly solution to the problem of the sin of the world. Told like that, the incarnation is a rescue mission for a world in crisis. Does it mean that if we had not sinned, we would never have met Jesus? Would Christmas never have happened?

We are right to emphasize the seriousness of sin. A faith with a cross at its centre will never underestimate the depths from which all this needs redeeming. But the focus is too narrow. Sin and salvation are part of a bigger picture. The incarnation was part of God's great, eternal plan all along. 'The Incarnation needs to be put back into the whole scheme of creation,' writes Orthodox theologian Olivier Clement:

> Human waywardness has certainly transformed it into a tragic redemption, but the Incarnation remains above all the fulfilment of God's original plan, the great synthesis, in Christ, of the human, the divine and the cosmic – 'he is before all things and in him all things hold together' (Col. 1.16–17). Everything exists in an immense movement of incarnation which tends towards Christ and is fulfilled in him. (2015, pp. 38–9)

This is all so much more than a story of sin to redemption. This is about creation to deification. 'God became incarnate that we might become God' was St Athanasius' bold expressing of it. We become 'participants in the divine nature' is St Peter's way of expressing this (2 Pet. 1.3–4).

The joyful declarations in the Easter night liturgy celebrate this revelation using quite startlingly intimate imagery.

> This is the night when Jesus Christ vanquished hell,
> broke the chains of death
> and rose triumphant from the grave.

> Most blessed of all nights!
> When wickedness is put to flight
> and sin is washed away,
> lost innocence regained, and mourning turned to joy.

Night, truly blessed,
when heaven is wedded to us,
and all creation, reconciled to God!
(*Lent, Holy Week, Easter Services and Prayers*, 1986,
London: Church House Publishing, p. 231)

God's desire was always that the world should exist so that
it might enter into his joy. We are his beloved. Christ is the
bridegroom, we – the world – his bride. The tomb has become
a bridal chamber. 'Resurrection is the consummation of the
marriage of heaven and earth' (Williams, 2014, p. 34). The
journey is not back to the garden. The story of creation was
always looking beyond itself. Humanity, in Christ, is united
with God in love, and God with us. God's desire, and ours, is
fulfilled, 'that we may evermore dwell in him and he in us'.

I love the early Easter morning service. The anticipation as
we gather in the cold and dark before the dawn. The first flame
is kindled – 'Let there be light!' Genesis chapter 1 is read. 'In the
beginning' ... and in the sequence of rituals, music and liturgy
that follows, all the primal elements of the first creation are
invoked. It is all beginning over again, in the resurrection life
of Christ.

The service continues, telling the story of original gift, fall,
and the steady descent of the world into sin and death. Then
of the coming of Jesus into the world, of his love, suffering and
dying. The liturgy is building up to a climax until the sin of
Adam is actually eclipsed by the overwhelming glory of what
is now revealed through the cross of Christ, concluding with
the astonishing cry – 'O happy fault that won for us so great a
salvation!'

This all continues as it first began. At unimaginable cost and
with inexhaustible mercy, even human rebellion and betrayal
becomes the means by which God furthers his original creating
purpose. Our sin draws from God an even greater revelation of
his glory. Beyond all hope, the life that began in a garden will
be completed in the fullness of the life of God.

O happy fault!

Praying in the Dust

Give me a candle of the spirit, O God
as I go down into the deep of my own being.
Show me the hidden things.
Take me down to the spring of my life, and
tell me my nature and my name.
Give me freedom to grow so that I
may become my true self – the
fulfilment of the seed which you
planted in me at my making.
Out of the deep I cry unto thee, O God.
Amen.

(George Appleton
adapted by Jim Cotter, 1985, p. 55)

Sources and Further Reading

Alexander, Denis, 2008, *Creation or Evolution: Do We Have to Choose?*, Oxford: Monarch.

——, 2010, 'Genetics, Theology, and Adam as a Historical Person', *BioLogos*, 16 December, https://biologos.org/articles/genetics-theology-and-adam-as-a-historical-person/, accessed 12.07.2024.

Alter, Robert, 1998, *Genesis – Translation & Commentary*, New York: W. W. Norton & Company.

——, 2011, *The Art of Biblical Narrative*, New York: Basic Press.

Archbishops' Council, 2000, *Common Worship*, London: Church House Publishing.

Atkinson, David, 2008, *Renewing the Face of the Earth – A Theological and Pastoral Response to Climate Change*, Norwich: Canterbury Press.

Atwell, Robert, 2011, *The Contented Life*, Norwich: Canterbury Press.

BioLogos, https://biologos.org, accessed 24.07.2024.

Brown, William, 2014, *Wisdom's Wonder – Character, Creation, and the Crisis in the Bible Wisdom Literature*, Grand Rapids, MI: Eerdmans.

Brueggemann, Walter, 2017, *Sabbath as Resistance*, Louisville, KY: Westminster John Knox Press.

——, 2021, *An Introduction to the Old Testament: The Canon and Christian Imagination*, Louisville, KY: Westminster John Knox Press.

Clement, Olivier, 2015, *The Roots of Christian Mysticism*, London: New City.

Collier, Winn, 2021, *A Burning in My Bones: The Authorized Biography of Eugene Peterson*, Milton Keynes: Authentic Media.

Collins, Francis, 2007, *The Language of God: A Scientist Presents Evidence for Belief*, London: Simon & Schuster.

Cotter, Jim, 1985, *Prayer at Night*, Sheffield: Cairns Publications.

Davis, Dick, 1988, *Thomas Traherne – Selected Writings*, Manchester: Carcanet.

Davis, Ellen, 2004, *Proverbs, Ecclesiastes, Song of Songs*, Louisville, KY: Westminster.

——, 2008, *Scripture, Culture and Agriculture – an agrarian reading of the Bible*, Cambridge: Cambridge University Press.

——, 2019, *Opening Israel's Scriptures*, Oxford: Oxford University Press.

Dowell, Graham, 1990, *Enjoying the World – The Rediscovery of Thomas Traherne*, London: Mowbray.

Elphinstone, Andrew, 1976, *Freedom, Suffering and Love*, London: SCM Press.

Fretheim, Terence E., 2010, *Creation Untamed – The Bible, God, and Natural Disasters*, Grand Rapids, MI: Baker Academic.

Goldingay, John, 2000, *Men Behaving Badly*, Milton Keynes: Paternoster Press.

———, 2010a, *Genesis for Everyone*, London: SPCK.

———, 2010b, *Proverbs for Everyone*, London: SPCK.

Greenblatt, Stephen, 2017, *The Rise and Fall of Adam and Eve – The Story that Created Us*, London: Vintage.

Guppy, Shusha, 1996, 'Amos Oz, The Art of Fiction No. 148', *The Paris Review*, 140 (Fall), https://www.theparisreview.org/interviews/1366/the-art-of-fiction-no-148-amos-oz, accessed 12.07.2024.

Haarsma, Loren, 2021, *When Did Sin Begin? – Human Evolution and the Doctrine of Original Sin*, Grand Rapids, MI: Baker Academic.

Hays, Richard B. and Davis, Ellen, F. (eds), 2003, *The Art of Reading Scripture*, Grand Rapids, MI: Eerdmans.

Holewinski, Britt, 'Underground Networking: The Amazing Connections Beneath Your Feet', *National Forest Foundation*, https://www.nationalforests.org/blog/underground-mycorrhizal-network, accessed 12.07.2024.

Keen, Karen R., 2022, *The Word of a Humble God – The Origins, Inspiration, and Interpretation of Scripture*, Grand Rapids, MI: Eerdmans.

Kuhn, Karl A., 2008, *Having Words with God – The Bible as Conversation*, Minneapolis, MN: Fortress Press.

Lewis, C. S., 1950, *The Lion, the Witch and the Wardrobe*, London: Penguin.

Louth, Andrew, 2013, *Introducing Easter Orthodox Theology*, Lisle, IL: IVP Academic.

Marshall, I. Howard, 2004, *Beyond the Bible – Moving from Scripture to Theology*, Grand Rapids, MI: Baker Academic.

Merton, Thomas, 1964, *Raids on the Unspeakable*, New York: New Directions.

———, 1972, *New Seeds of Contemplation*, New York: Anthony Clark.

Moltmann, Jürgen, 1981, *The Trinity and the Kingdom of God*, London: SCM Press.

Moore, Gareth, 2003, *A Question of Truth*, London: Continuum.

Murphy, F., 2001, *The Comedy of Revelation Paradise – Lost and Regained in Biblical Narrative*, Edinburgh: T&T Clark.

Ramsey, A. M., 2012, *God, Christ and the World*, London: SCM Press.

Reymo, Chet, 1985, *The Soul of the Night – An Astronomical Pilgrimage*, Hoboken, NJ: Prentice Hall.

Richards, Anne, and the Mission Theology Advisory Group, 2017,

'The Five Marks of Mission', https://www.churchofengland.org/sites/default/files/2017-11/mtag-the-5-marks-of-mission.pdf, accessed 12.07.2024.

Runcorn, David, 1990, *Space for God, Silence and Solitude in the Christian Life*, London: Darton, Longman and Todd.

———, 2003, *Choice, Desire and the Will of God: What More Do You Want?*, London: SPCK.

———, 2008, *Creation of Adam – Seven Guided Reflections from Genesis*, Cambridge: Grove Books.

———, 2011, *Fear and Trust – God-centred Leadership*, London: SPCK.

———, 2020, *Love Means Love – Same-sex Relationships and the Bible*, London: SPCK.

Sacks, Jonathan, 2009, *Covenant & Conversation: Genesis*, Oxford: Oxford University Press.

Slimak, Ludovic, 2024, *The Naked Neanderthal*, London: Penguin.

Spufford, Francis, 2013, *Unapologetic – Why, Despite Everything, Christianity Can Still Make Surprising Emotional Sense*, London: Faber and Faber.

Suurmond, Jean-Jacques, 1994, *Word and Spirit at Play*, London: SCM Press.

Taylor, John V., 1992, *The Christlike God*, London: SCM Press.

Taylor, M., 2024, *Impossible Monsters – Dinosaurs, Darwin and the War Between Science and Religion*, New York: Vintage.

Tippett, Krista, 2005, 'John Polkinghorne: Quarks and Creation', *On Being*, 10 March, https://onbeing.org/programs/john-polkinghorne-quarks-and-creation/, accessed 12.07.2024.

Tomkins, Stephen, 2013, 'Francis Spufford interview: Clear Christianity', *Reform Magazine*, June, https://www.reform-magazine.co.uk/2013/05/clear-christianity/, accessed 12.07.2024 .

Triduum Sourcebook, 1983, Diocese of Chicago.

Vanstone, W. H., 1977, *Love's Endeavour, Love's Expense*, London: Darton, Longman and Todd.

Von Rad, Gerhard, 1972, *Genesis*, London: SCM Press.

Waddell, Helen, 1950, *Peter Abelard*, London: The Reprint Society.

Warner, Meg, 2024, *Genesis: An Introduction and Study Guide: A Past for a People in Need of a Future*, London: T&T Clark.

Wells, Samuel, 2018, *Improvisation – The drama of Christian ethics*, Grand Rapids, MI: Baker Academic.

Williams, Harry, 1965, *True Wilderness*, London: Constable.

Williams, Rowan, 2014, *Resurrection*, London: Darton, Longman and Todd.

Wirzba, Norman, 2021, *This Sacred Life – Humanity's Place in a Wounded World*, Cambridge: Cambridge University Press.

Acknowledgements

I have been exploring the themes in this book in many different contexts over a number of years – through retreats, Bible studies, preaching, theological study days, blogs and in many personal conversations. These included times of specific focus on the Genesis passages, but the discussions constantly broadened to reflect on how to read and interpret the Bible revelation as a whole. So, a wide and general thank you is due to the many groups and individuals who have made this such a consistently nurturing resource for my own faith and understanding. In my introduction I mentioned participants on the Scargill House holiday week in November 2023. The decision to turn these themes into a book was first suggested there.

My thanks to my publisher Christine Smith for supporting the idea, and for the pleasure of writing for Canterbury Press again.

Special thanks to the Inclusive Evangelicals network, our Facebook group and the convenor group I am part of. Their fellowship, stimulation, courage, honesty, adventurous faith and love of scripture is a constant joy and challenge. Particular thanks to Isabelle Hamley and Karen Keen for significantly resourcing my wider reflections on scripture. Richard Cooke, Greg Bakker, Tim Chesterton and David Newman read drafts at different stages and gave wise and astute feedback. Simon Kingston has once again been my critical companion as the book has emerged. Over the years, as a writer, I owe him more than I can say.

Biggest thanks to Jackie my wife (and bishop), my dearest friend, theological foil and companion in the pilgrimage of life and ministry. And to my dear family, Josh, Leona, Simeon and Kate for their love, enthusiasm and constant encouragement.

The Bible Texts

The first creation story: Genesis 1 – 2.3

In the beginning when God created the heavens and the earth, [2] the earth was a formless void and darkness covered the face of the deep, while a wind from God swept over the face of the waters. [3] Then God said, 'Let there be light'; and there was light. [4] And God saw that the light was good; and God separated the light from the darkness. [5] God called the light Day, and the darkness he called Night. And there was evening and there was morning, the first day.

[6] And God said, 'Let there be a dome in the midst of the waters, and let it separate the waters from the waters.' [7] So God made the dome and separated the waters that were under the dome from the waters that were above the dome. And it was so. [8] God called the dome Sky. And there was evening and there was morning, the second day.

[9] And God said, 'Let the waters under the sky be gathered together into one place, and let the dry land appear.' And it was so. [10] God called the dry land Earth, and the waters that were gathered together he called Seas. And God saw that it was good. [11] Then God said, 'Let the earth put forth vegetation: plants yielding seed, and fruit trees of every kind on earth that bear fruit with the seed in it.' And it was so. [12] The earth brought forth vegetation: plants yielding seed of every kind, and trees of every kind bearing fruit with the seed in it. And God saw that it was good. [13] And there was evening and there was morning, the third day.

[14] And God said, 'Let there be lights in the dome of the sky to separate the day from the night; and let them be for signs and for seasons and for days and years, [15] and let them be lights in

the dome of the sky to give light upon the earth.' And it was so. [16] God made the two great lights — the greater light to rule the day and the lesser light to rule the night — and the stars. [17] God set them in the dome of the sky to give light upon the earth, [18] to rule over the day and over the night, and to separate the light from the darkness. And God saw that it was good. [19] And there was evening and there was morning, the fourth day.

[20] And God said, 'Let the waters bring forth swarms of living creatures, and let birds fly above the earth across the dome of the sky.' [21] So God created the great sea monsters and every living creature that moves, of every kind, with which the waters swarm, and every winged bird of every kind. And God saw that it was good. [22] God blessed them, saying, 'Be fruitful and multiply and fill the waters in the seas, and let birds multiply on the earth.' [23] And there was evening and there was morning, the fifth day.

[24] And God said, 'Let the earth bring forth living creatures of every kind: cattle and creeping things and wild animals of the earth of every kind.' And it was so. [25] God made the wild animals of the earth of every kind, and the cattle of every kind, and everything that creeps upon the ground of every kind. And God saw that it was good.

[26] Then God said, 'Let us make humankind in our image, according to our likeness; and let them have dominion over the fish of the sea, and over the birds of the air, and over the cattle, and over all the wild animals of the earth, and over every creeping thing that creeps upon the earth.'

[27] So God created humankind in his image,
in the image of God he created them;
male and female he created them.

[28] God blessed them, and God said to them, 'Be fruitful and multiply, and fill the earth and subdue it; and have dominion over the fish of the sea and over the birds of the air and over every living thing that moves upon the earth.' [29] God said, 'See, I have given you every plant yielding seed that is upon the face of all the earth, and every tree with seed in its fruit; you shall have them for food. [30] And to every beast of the earth, and to every bird of the air, and to everything that creeps on the earth,

everything that has the breath of life, I have given every green plant for food.' And it was so. [31] God saw everything that he had made, and indeed, it was very good. And there was evening and there was morning, the sixth day.

2 [1] Thus the heavens and the earth were finished, and all their multitude. [2] And on the seventh day God finished the work that he had done, and he rested on the seventh day from all the work that he had done. [3] So God blessed the seventh day and hallowed it, because on it God rested from all the work that he had done in creation.

The second creation story: Genesis 2.4 – 3

In the day that the Lord God made the earth and the heavens, [5] when no plant of the field was yet in the earth and no herb of the field had yet sprung up — for the Lord God had not caused it to rain upon the earth, and there was no one to till the ground; [6] but a stream would rise from the earth, and water the whole face of the ground — [7] then the Lord God formed man from the dust of the ground, and breathed into his nostrils the breath of life; and the man became a living being. [8] And the Lord God planted a garden in Eden, in the east; and there he put the man whom he had formed. [9] Out of the ground the Lord God made to grow every tree that is pleasant to the sight and good for food, the tree of life also in the midst of the garden, and the tree of the knowledge of good and evil.

[10] A river flows out of Eden to water the garden, and from there it divides and becomes four branches. [11] The name of the first is Pishon; it is the one that flows around the whole land of Havilah, where there is gold; [12] and the gold of that land is good; bdellium and onyx stone are there. [13] The name of the second river is Gihon; it is the one that flows around the whole land of Cush. [14] The name of the third river is Tigris, which flows east of Assyria. And the fourth river is the Euphrates.

[15] The Lord God took the man and put him in the garden of Eden to till it and keep it. [16] And the Lord God commanded the man, 'You may freely eat of every tree of the garden; [17] but of

the tree of the knowledge of good and evil you shall not eat, for in the day that you eat of it you shall die.'

[18] Then the Lord God said, 'It is not good that the man should be alone; I will make him a helper as his partner.' [19] So out of the ground the Lord God formed every animal of the field and every bird of the air, and brought them to the man to see what he would call them; and whatever the man called each living creature, that was its name. [20] The man gave names to all cattle, and to the birds of the air, and to every animal of the field; but for the man there was not found a helper as his partner. [21] So the Lord God caused a deep sleep to fall upon the man, and he slept; then he took one of his ribs and closed up its place with flesh. [22] And the rib that the Lord God had taken from the man he made into a woman and brought her to the man. [23] Then the man said,

'This at last is bone of my bones
    and flesh of my flesh;
this one shall be called Woman,
    for out of Man this one was taken.'

[24] Therefore a man leaves his father and his mother and clings to his wife, and they become one flesh. [25] And the man and his wife were both naked, and were not ashamed.

3 Now the serpent was more crafty than any other wild animal that the Lord God had made. He said to the woman, 'Did God say, "You shall not eat from any tree in the garden"?' [2] The woman said to the serpent, 'We may eat of the fruit of the trees in the garden; [3] but God said, "You shall not eat of the fruit of the tree that is in the middle of the garden, nor shall you touch it, or you shall die."' [4] But the serpent said to the woman, 'You will not die; [5] for God knows that when you eat of it your eyes will be opened, and you will be like God, knowing good and evil.' [6] So when the woman saw that the tree was good for food, and that it was a delight to the eyes, and that the tree was to be desired to make one wise, she took of its fruit and ate; and she also gave some to her husband, who was with her, and he ate. [7] Then the eyes of both were opened, and they knew that they were naked; and they sewed fig leaves together and made loincloths for themselves.

⁸ They heard the sound of the Lord God walking in the garden at the time of the evening breeze, and the man and his wife hid themselves from the presence of the Lord God among the trees of the garden. ⁹ But the Lord God called to the man, and said to him, 'Where are you?' ¹⁰ He said, 'I heard the sound of you in the garden, and I was afraid, because I was naked; and I hid myself.' ¹¹ He said, 'Who told you that you were naked? Have you eaten from the tree of which I commanded you not to eat?' ¹² The man said, 'The woman whom you gave to be with me, she gave me fruit from the tree, and I ate.' ¹³ Then the Lord God said to the woman, 'What is this that you have done?' The woman said, 'The serpent tricked me, and I ate.' ¹⁴ The Lord God said to the serpent,

'Because you have done this,
cursed are you among all animals
and among all wild creatures;
upon your belly you shall go,
and dust you shall eat
all the days of your life.
¹⁵ I will put enmity between you and the woman,
and between your offspring and hers;
he will strike your head,
and you will strike his heel.'
¹⁶ To the woman he said,
'I will greatly increase your pangs in childbearing;
in pain you shall bring forth children,
yet your desire shall be for your husband,
and he shall rule over you.'
¹⁷ And to the man he said,
'Because you have listened to the voice of your wife,
and have eaten of the tree
about which I commanded you,
"You shall not eat of it",
cursed is the ground because of you;
in toil you shall eat of it all the days of your life
¹⁸ thorns and thistles it shall bring forth for you;
and you shall eat the plants of the field.
¹⁹ By the sweat of your face

you shall eat bread
until you return to the ground,
for out of it you were taken;
you are dust,
and to dust you shall return.'
²⁰ The man named his wife Eve, because she was the mother of all who live. ²¹ And the Lord God made garments of skins for the man and for his wife, and clothed them.

²² Then the Lord God said, 'See, the man has become like one of us, knowing good and evil; and now, he might reach out his hand and take also from the tree of life, and eat, and live for ever' — ²³ therefore the Lord God sent him forth from the garden of Eden, to till the ground from which he was taken. ²⁴ He drove out the man; and at the east of the garden of Eden he placed the cherubim, and a sword flaming and turning to guard the way to the tree of life.

www.ingramcontent.com/pod-product-compliance
Lightning Source LLC
LaVergne TN
LVHW040605211224
799547LV00006BA/74